COLORING BOOKS
FOR MEN
HUNTING

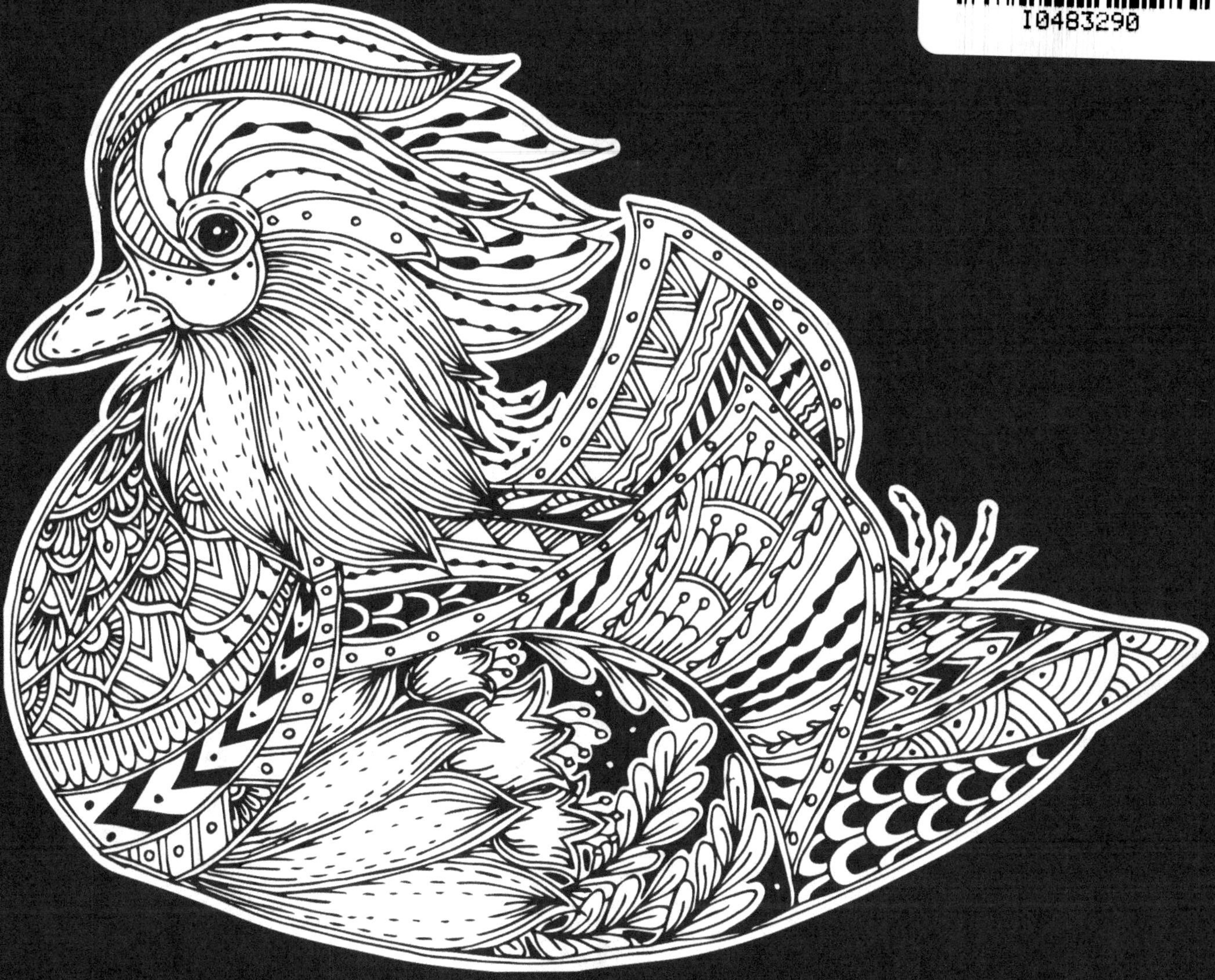

ART THERAPY COLORING

Preview of Coloring Pages

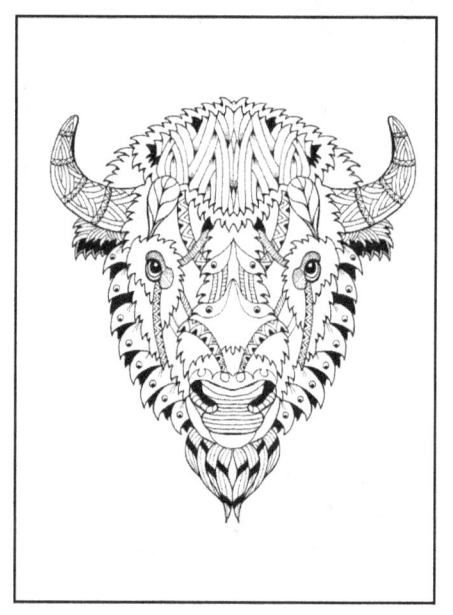
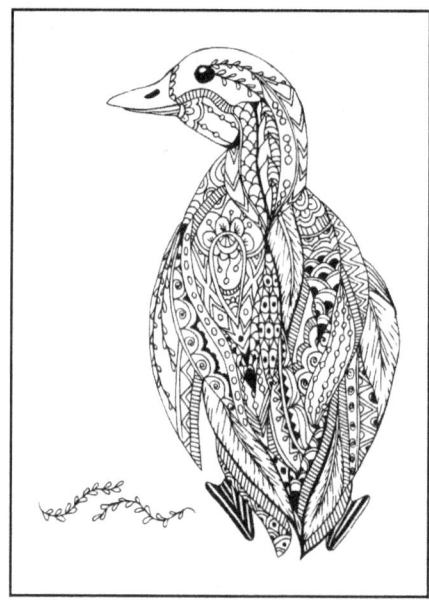
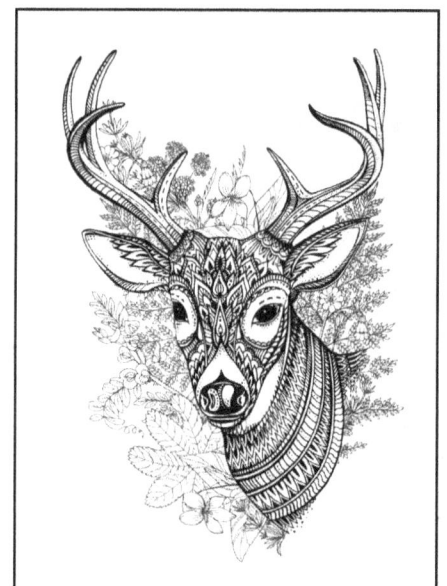
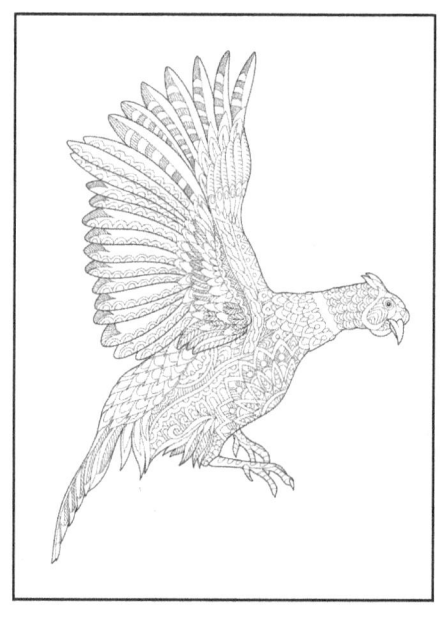
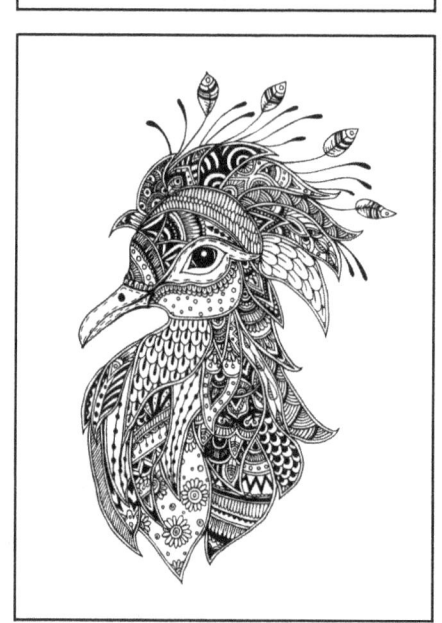
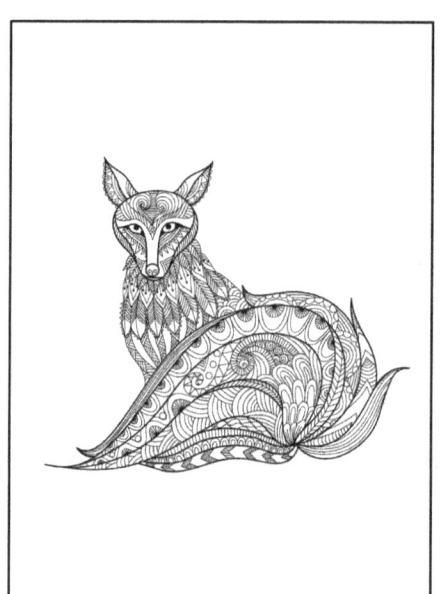
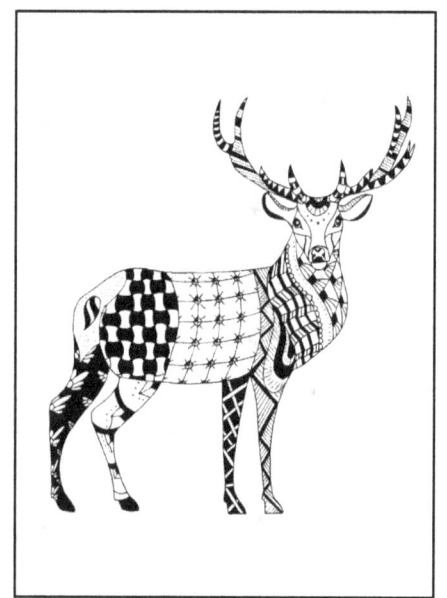
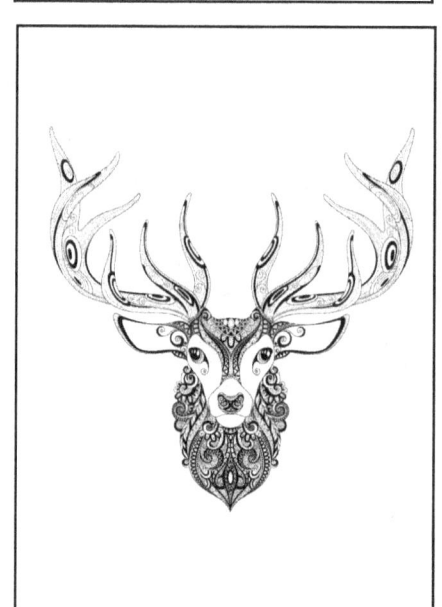
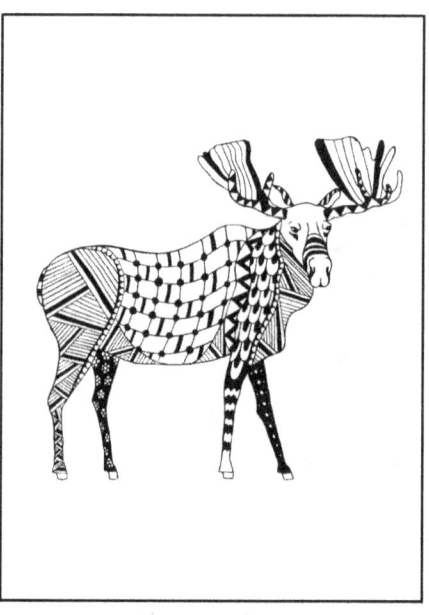

www.arttherapycoloring.com

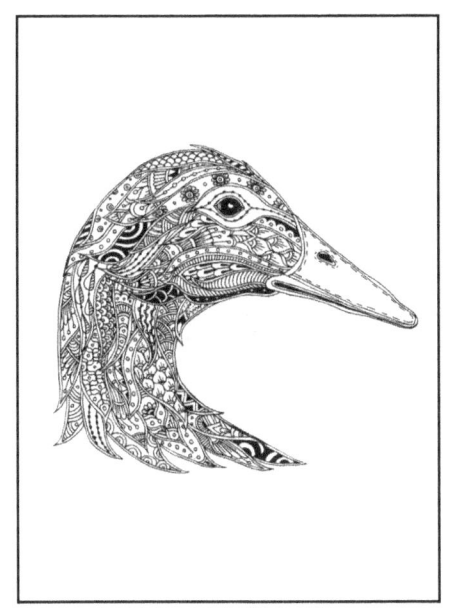
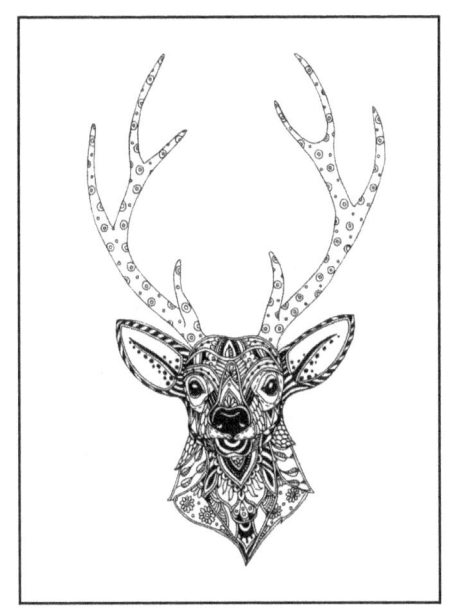
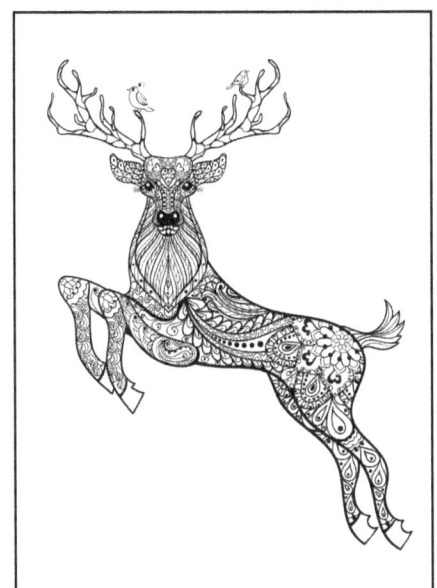
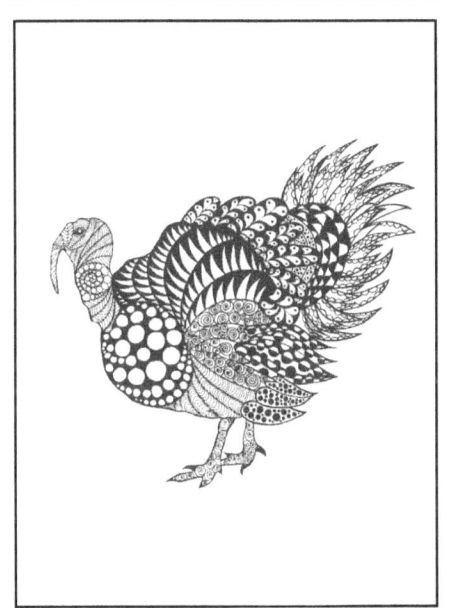
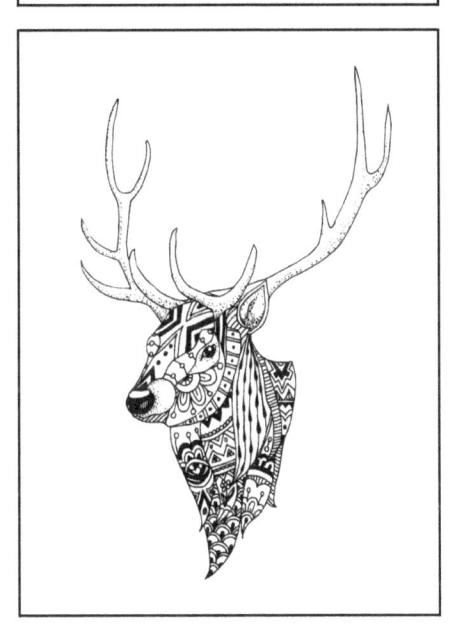
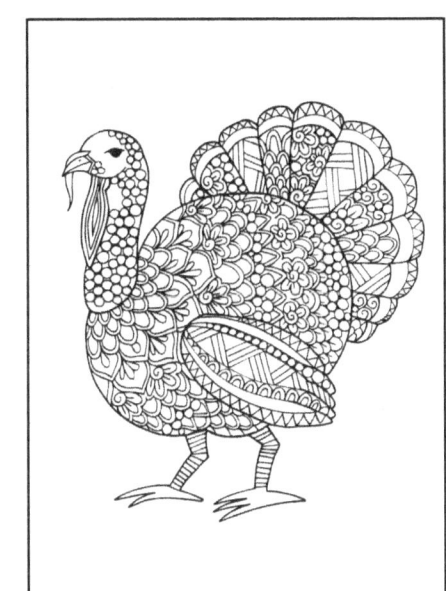
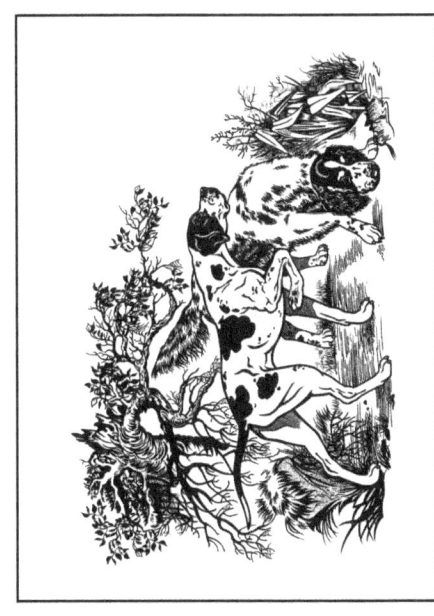
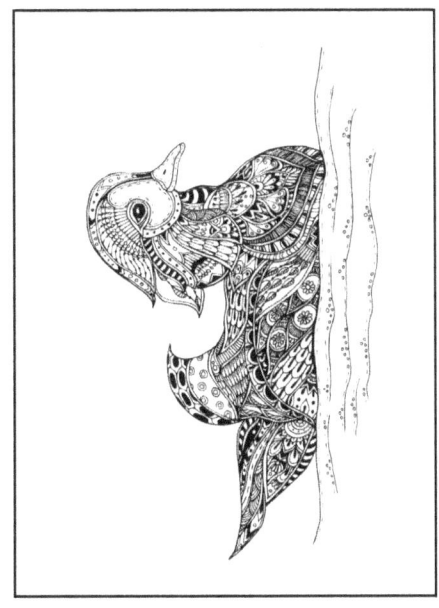
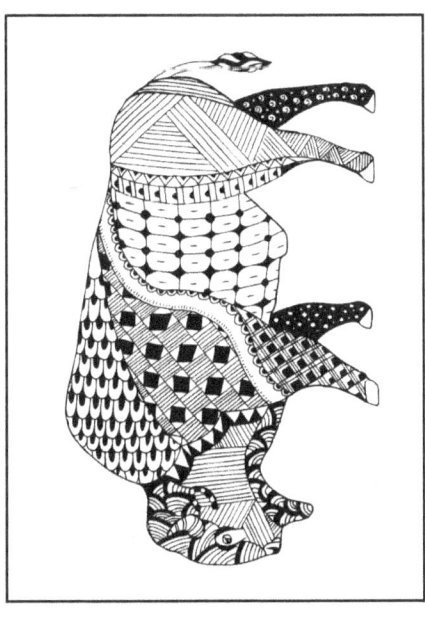

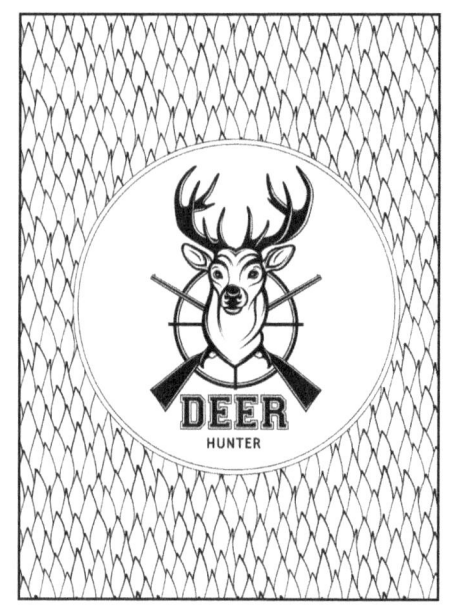

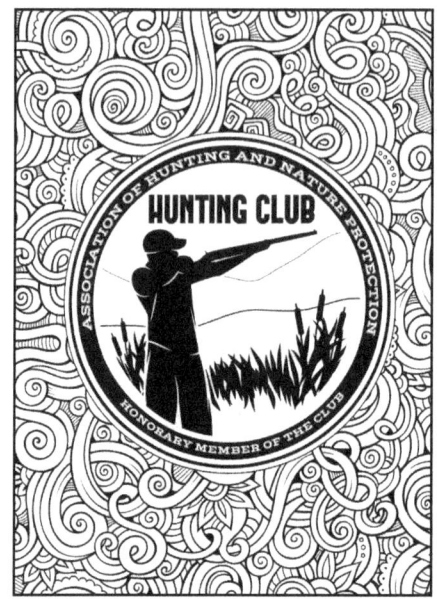

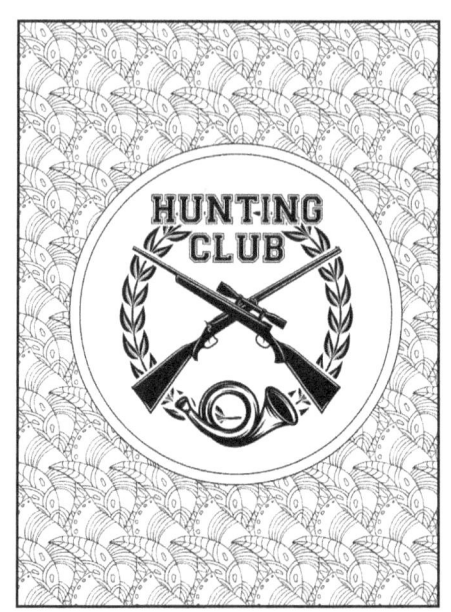

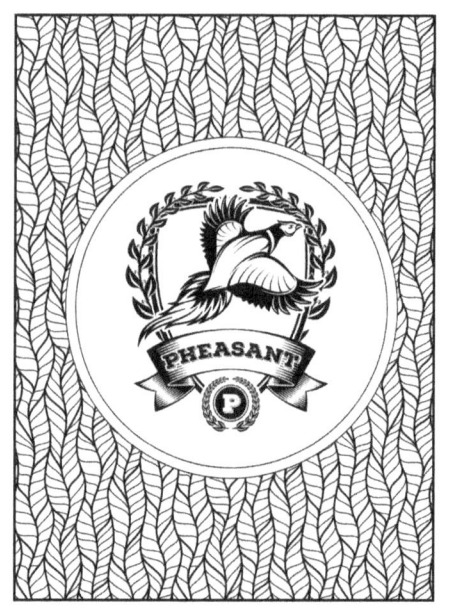

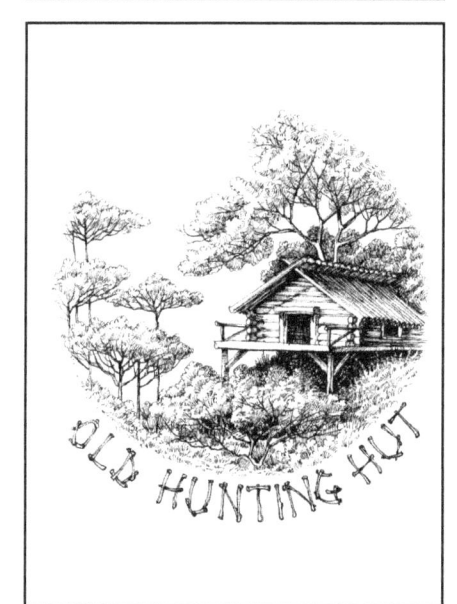

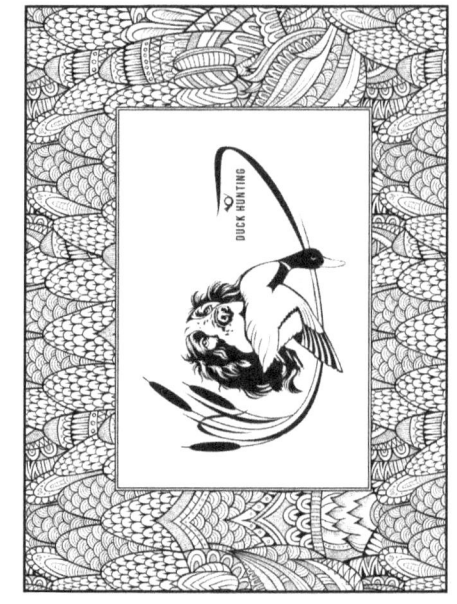

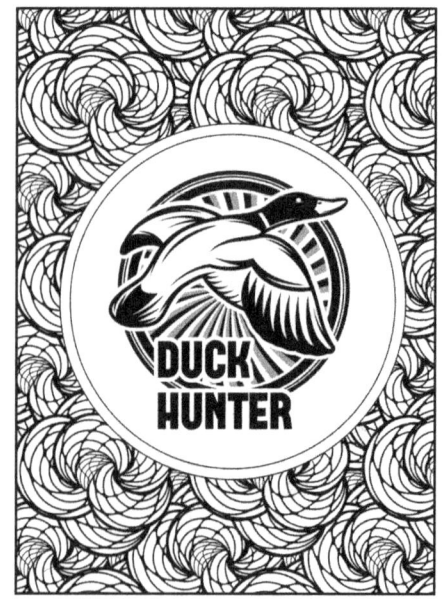

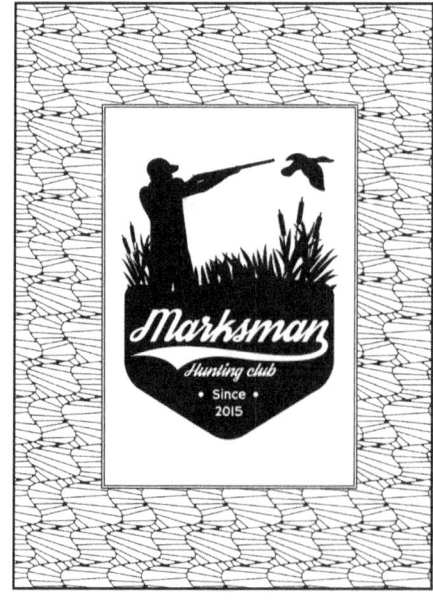

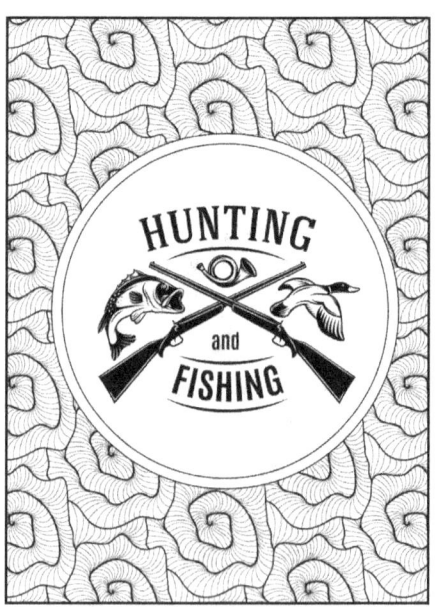

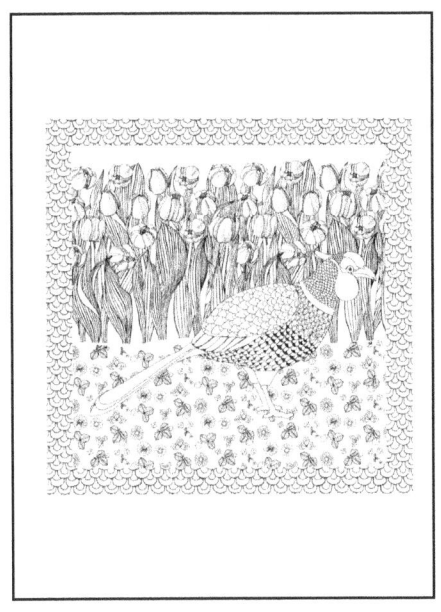
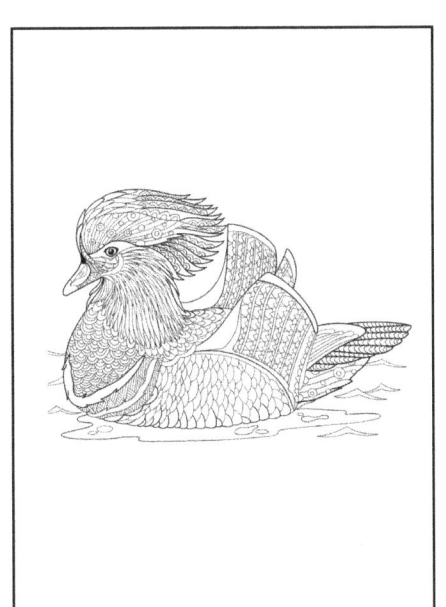
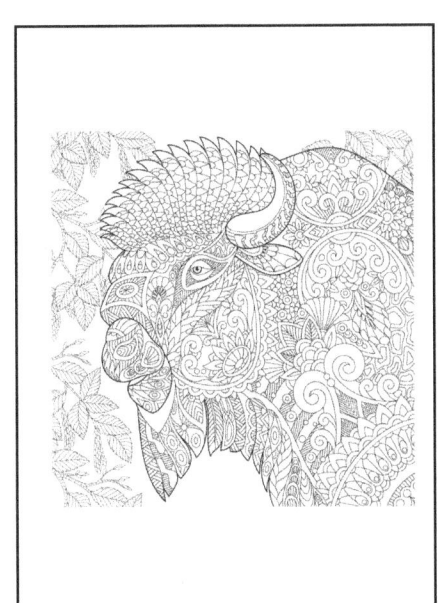
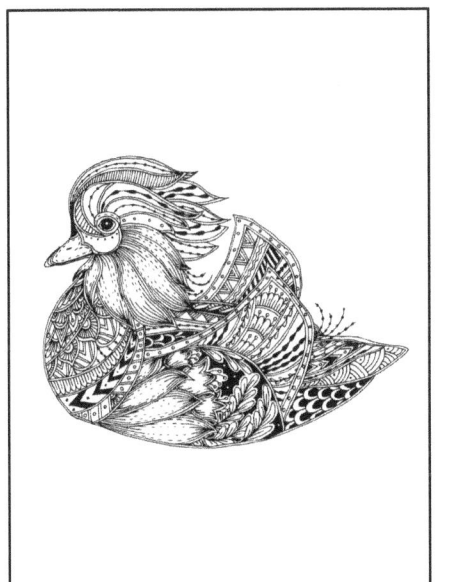
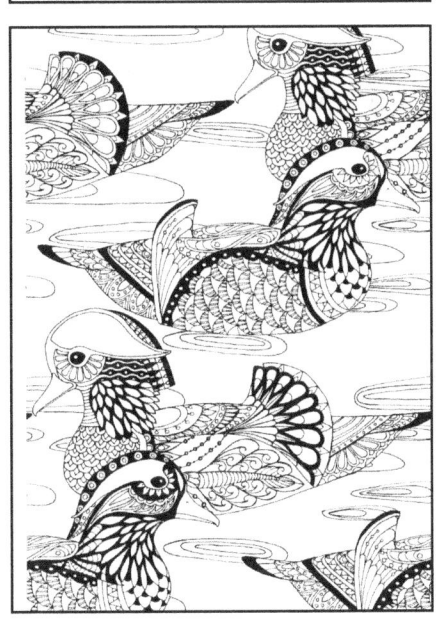
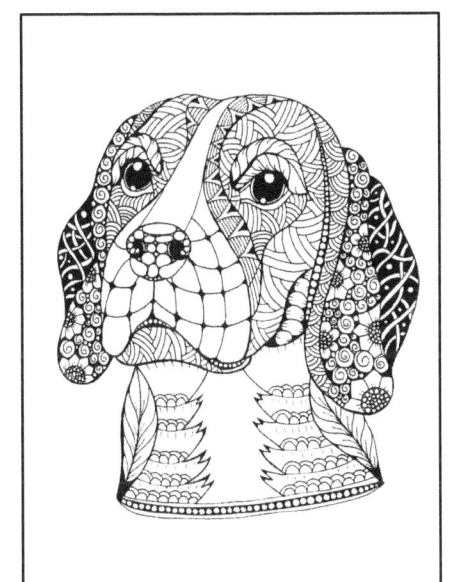
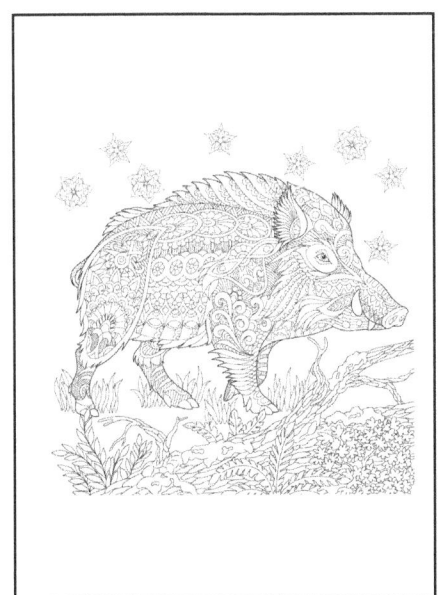
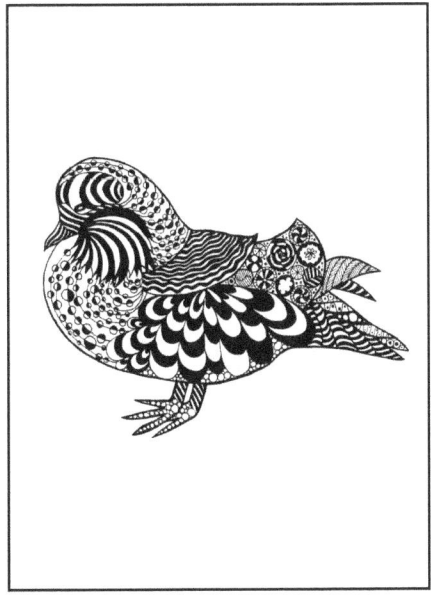
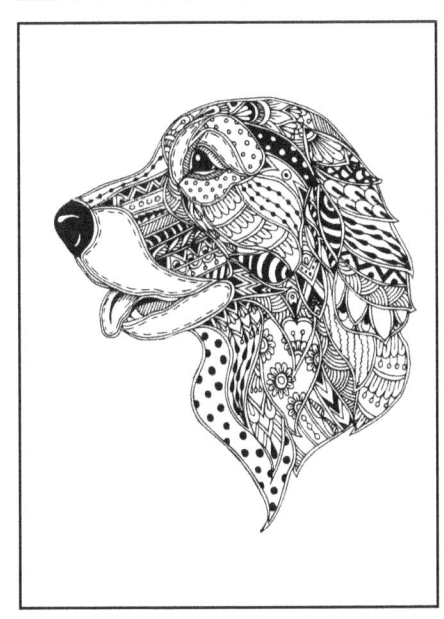

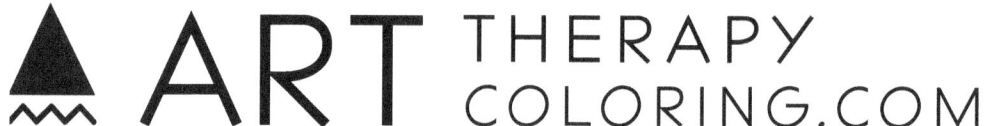

Did You Enjoy Our Coloring Book?

We Want To Hear About It!

Help spread the word about our adult coloring books! We give 10% of all proceeds from Art Therapy products to benefit pancreatic cancer patients and their families.

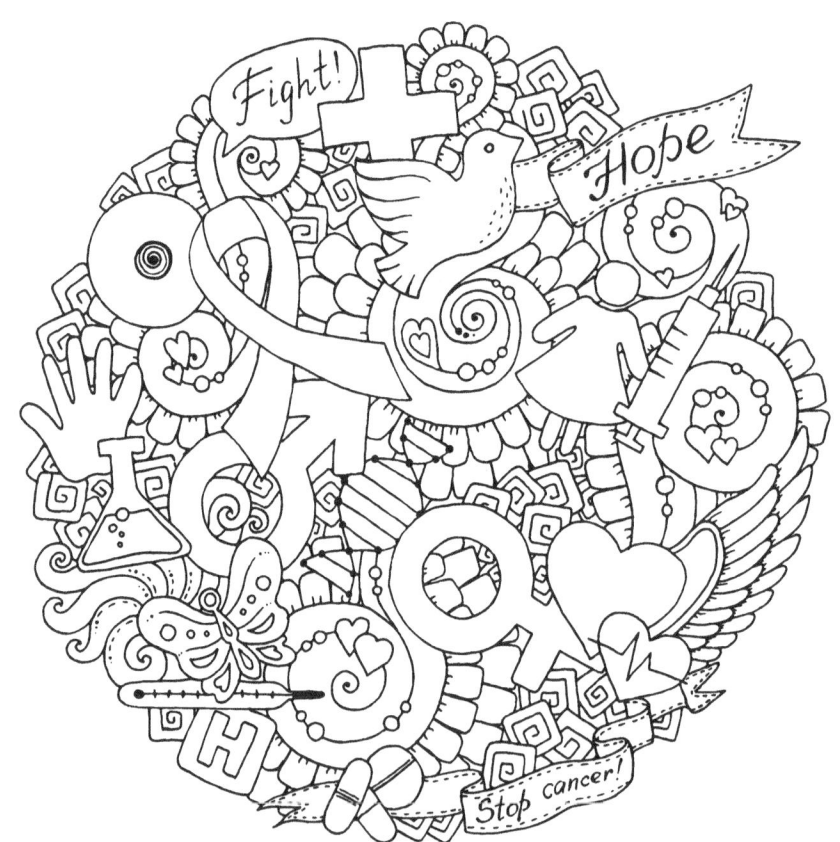

The best way to spread the word is through reviews. We know how busy you are, especially with all of that coloring, but we would appreciate it!

Visit our website at **www.arttherapycoloring.com**

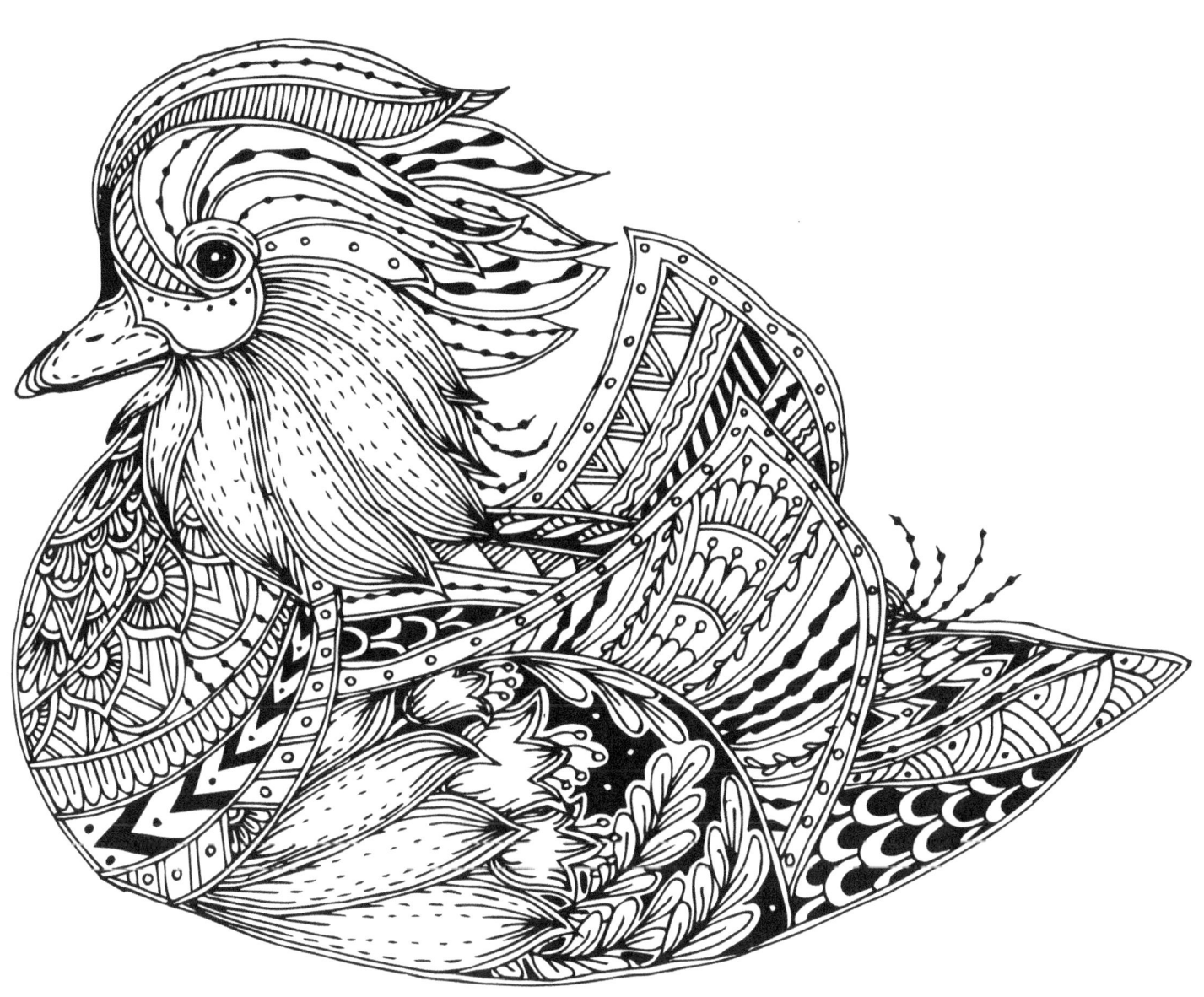

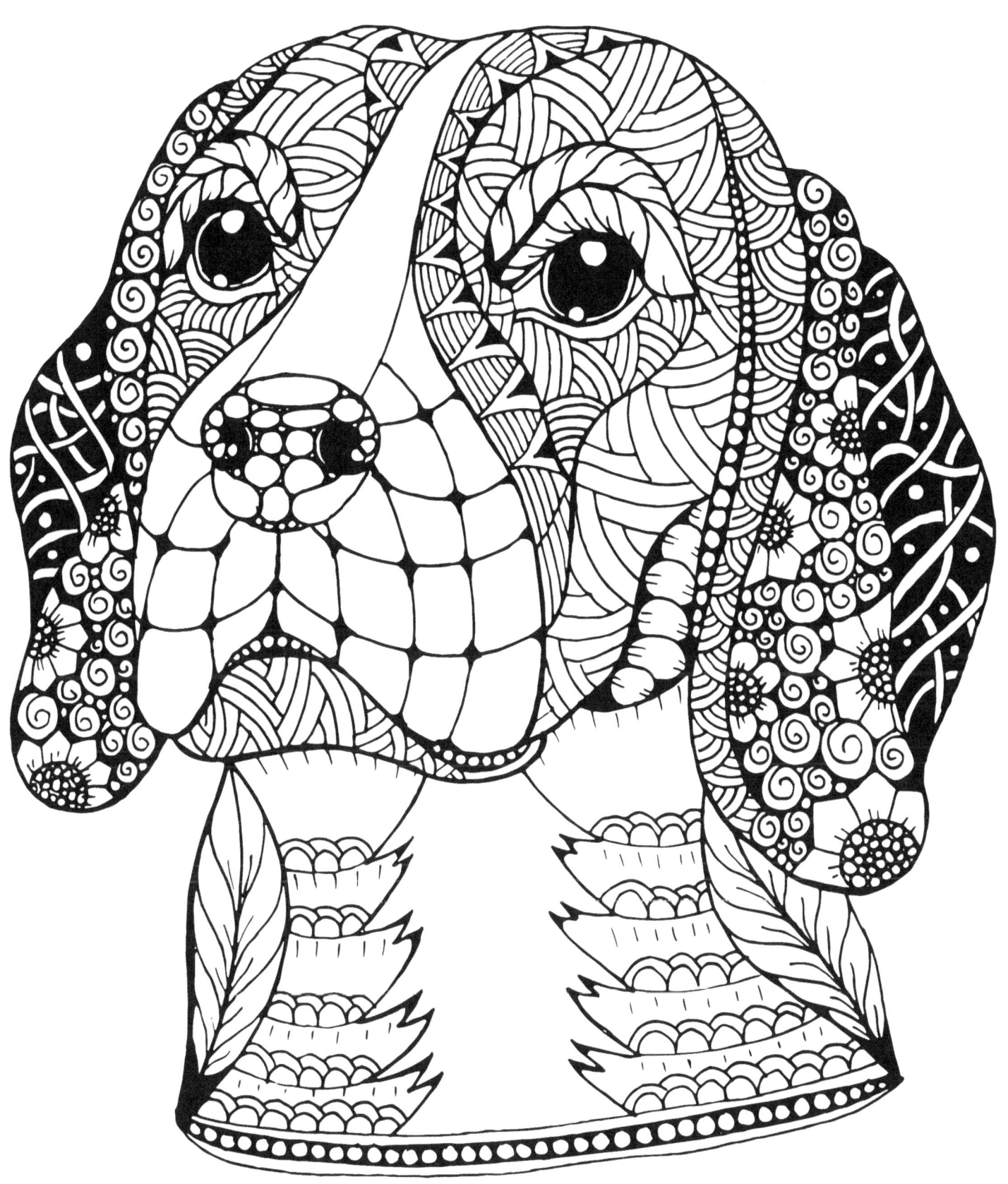

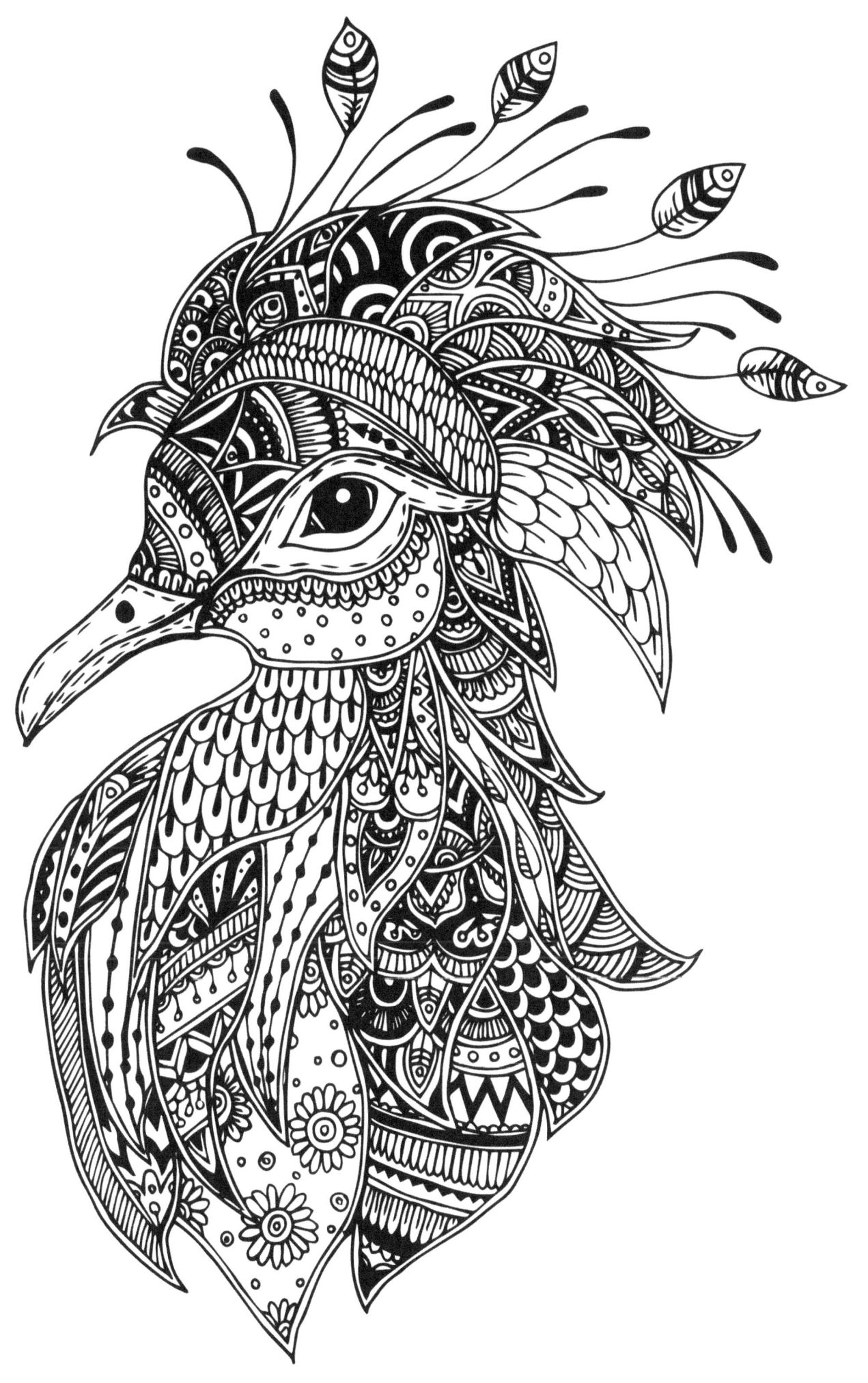

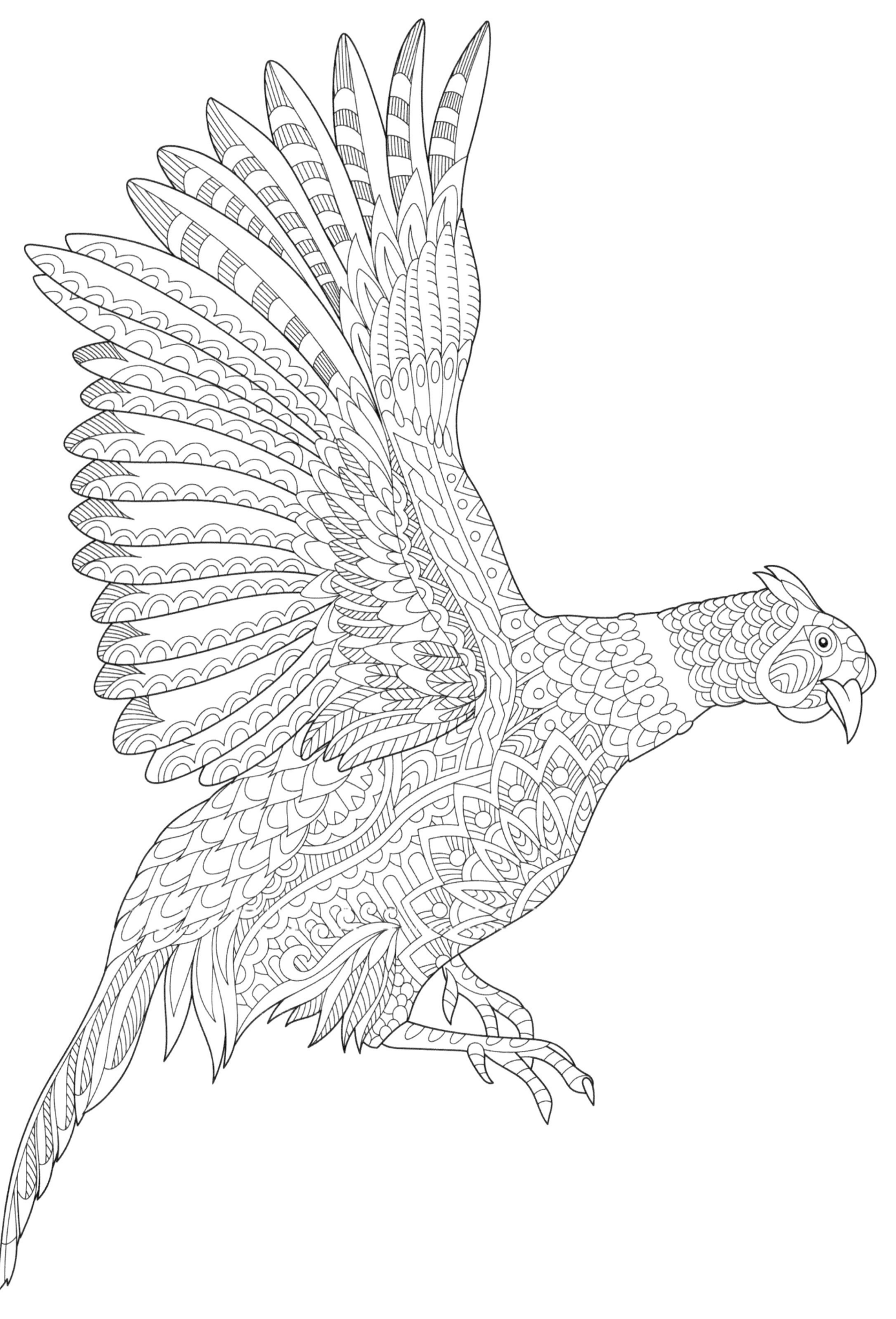

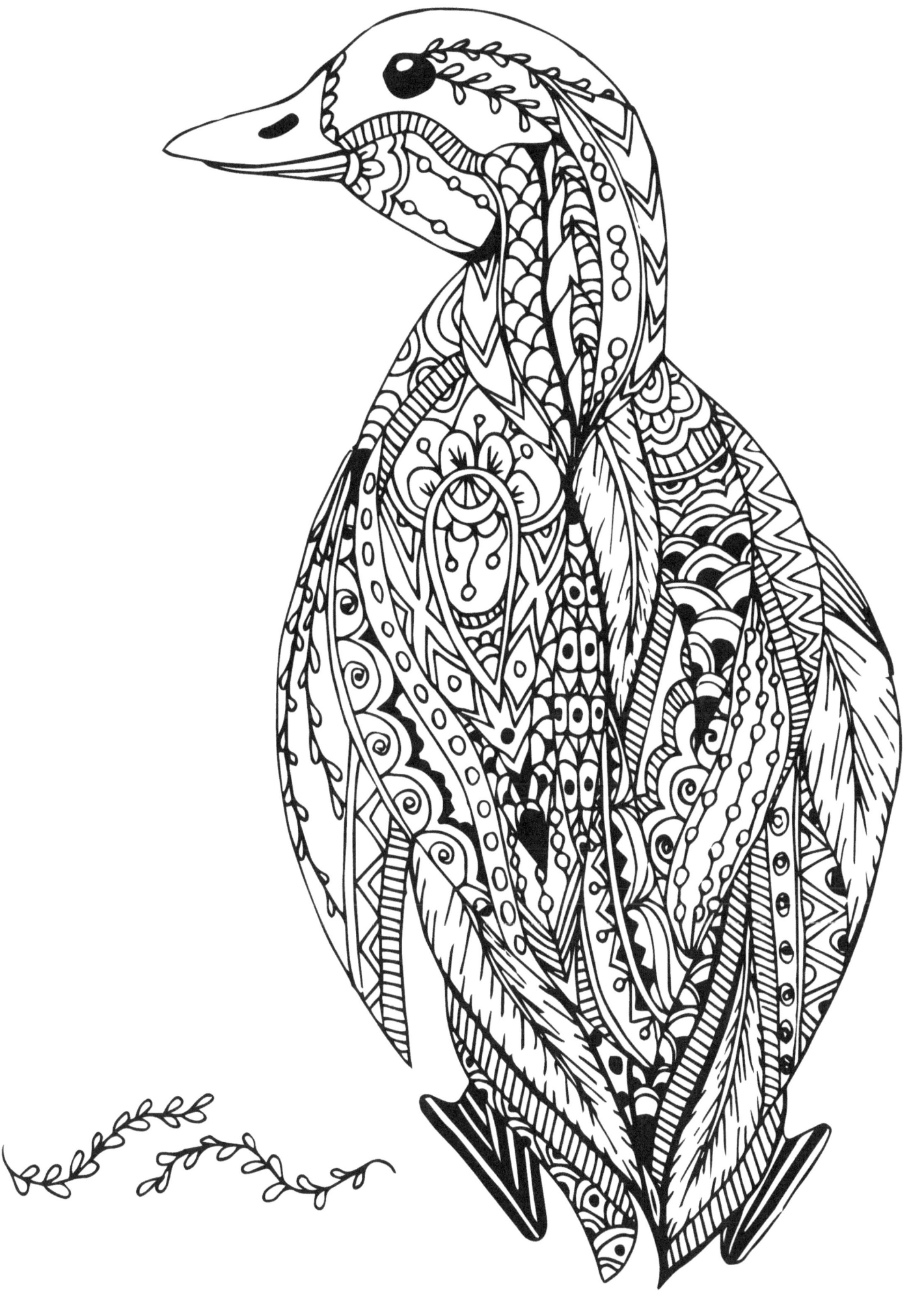

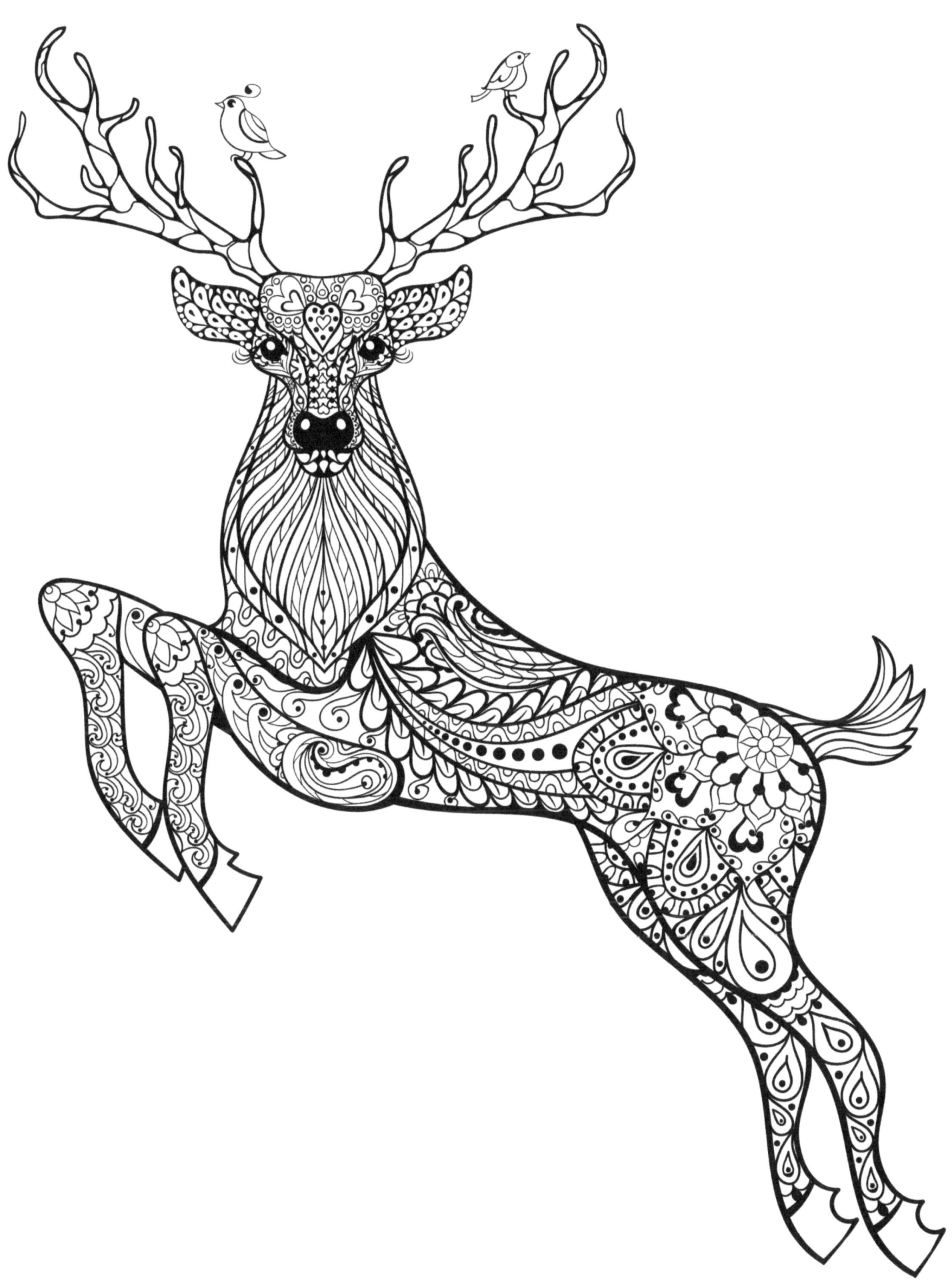

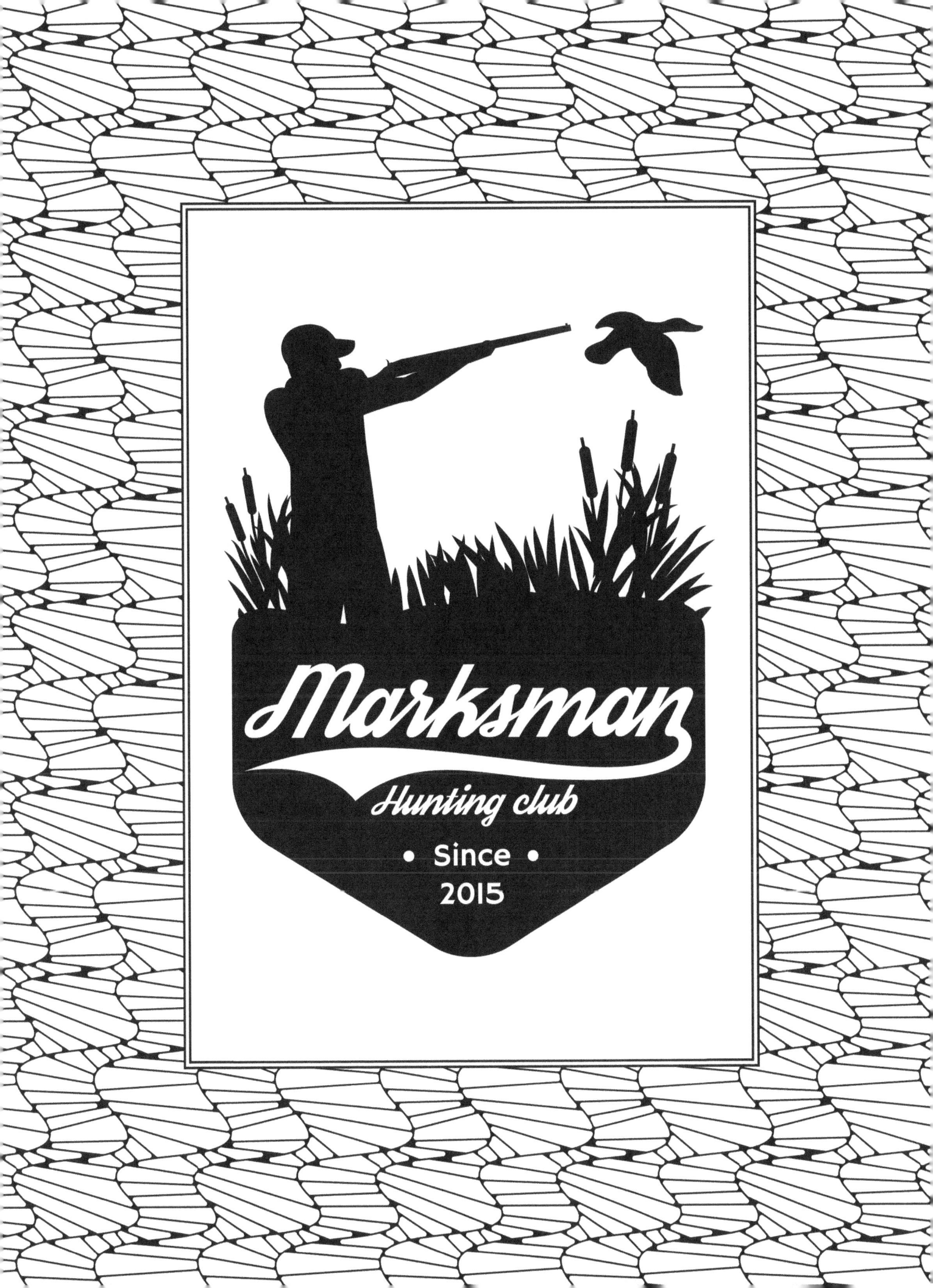

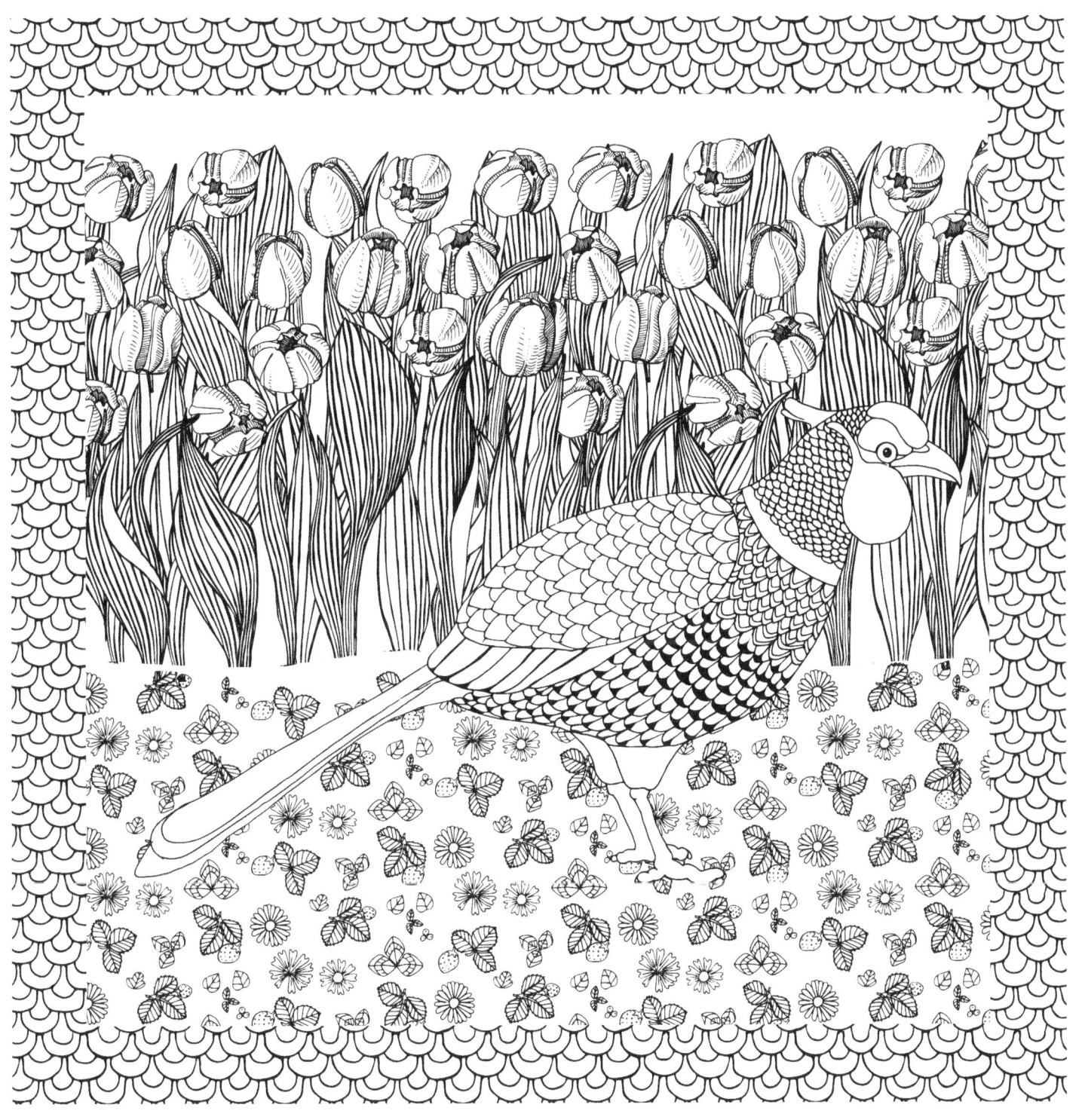

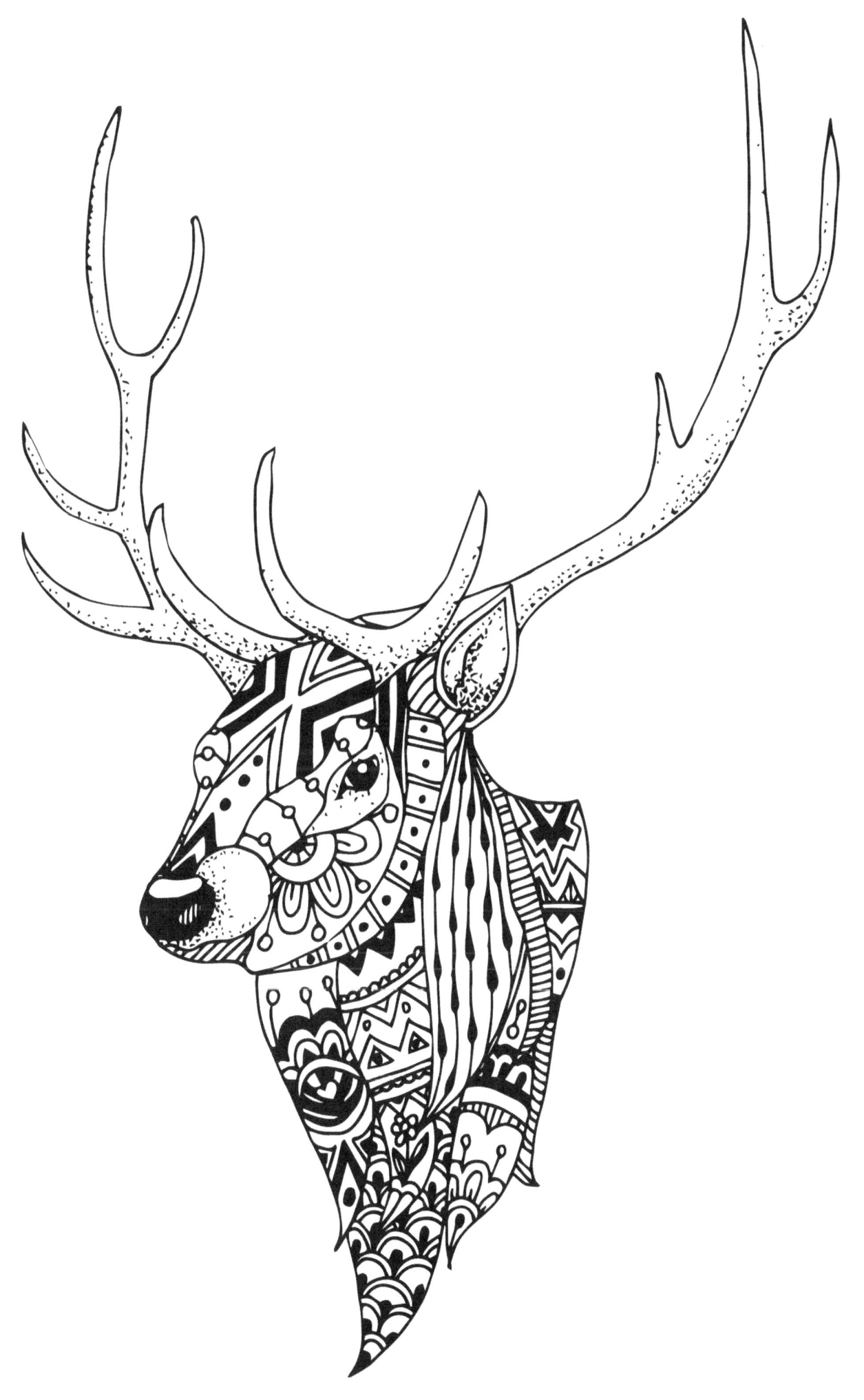

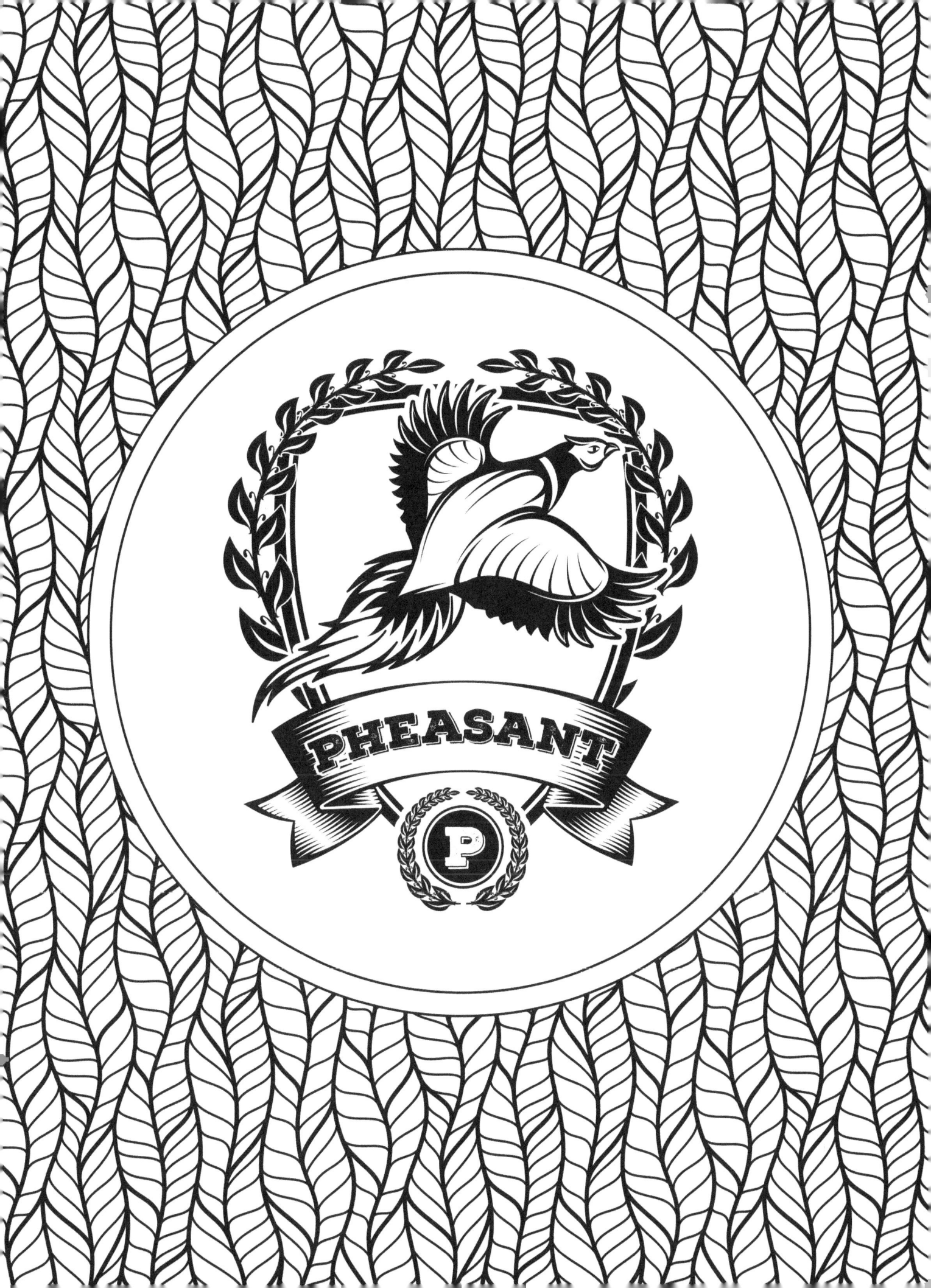

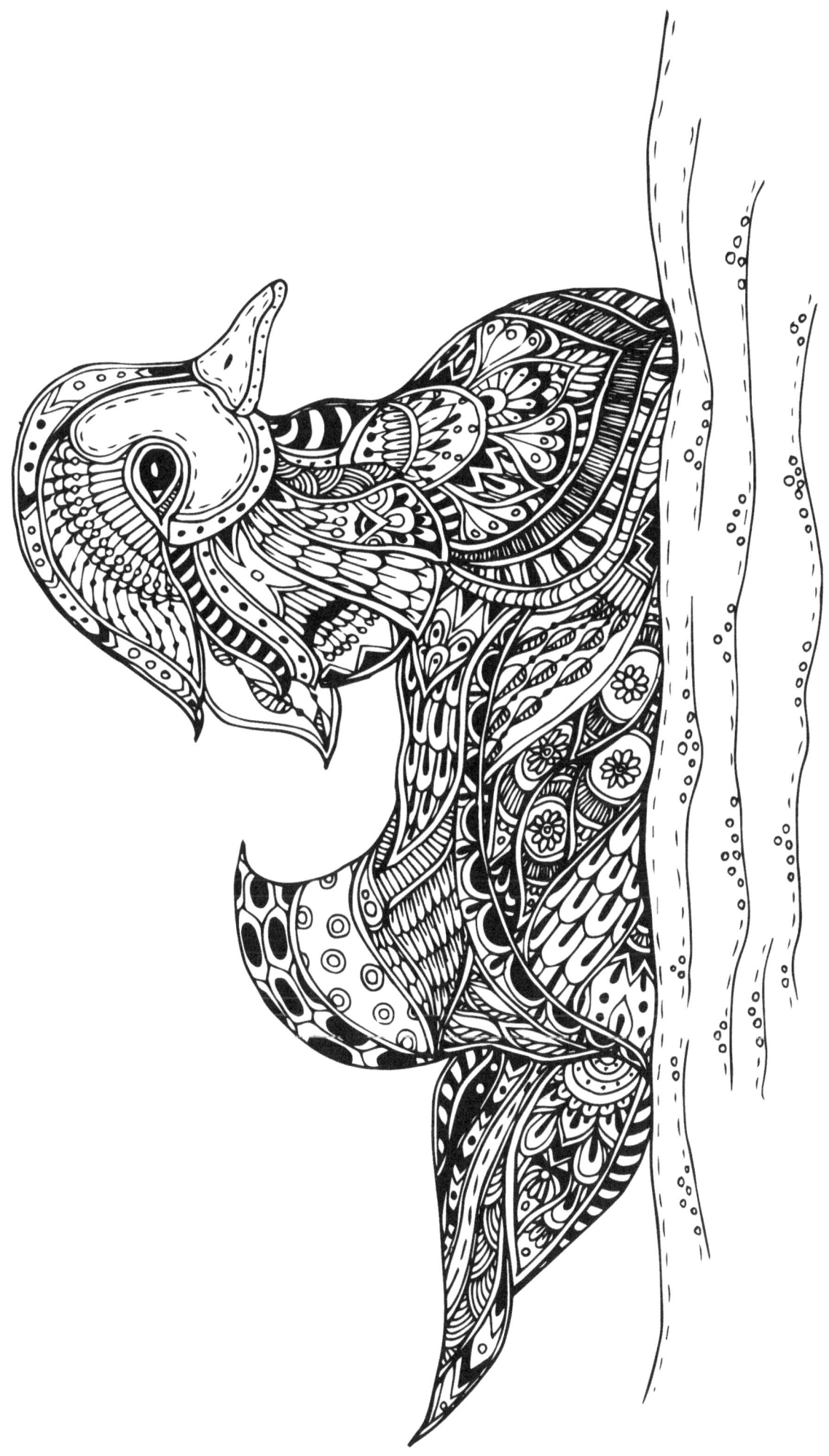

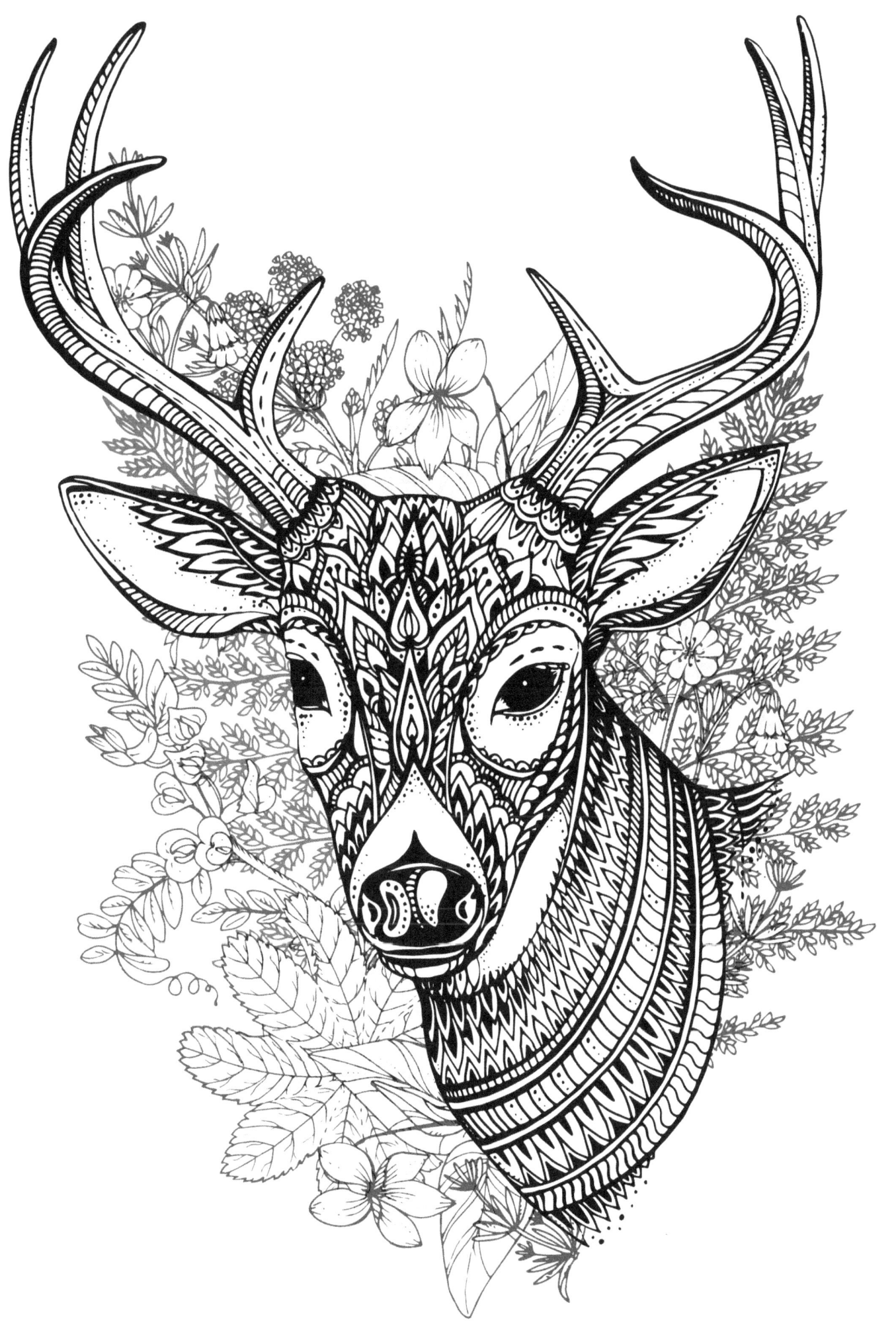

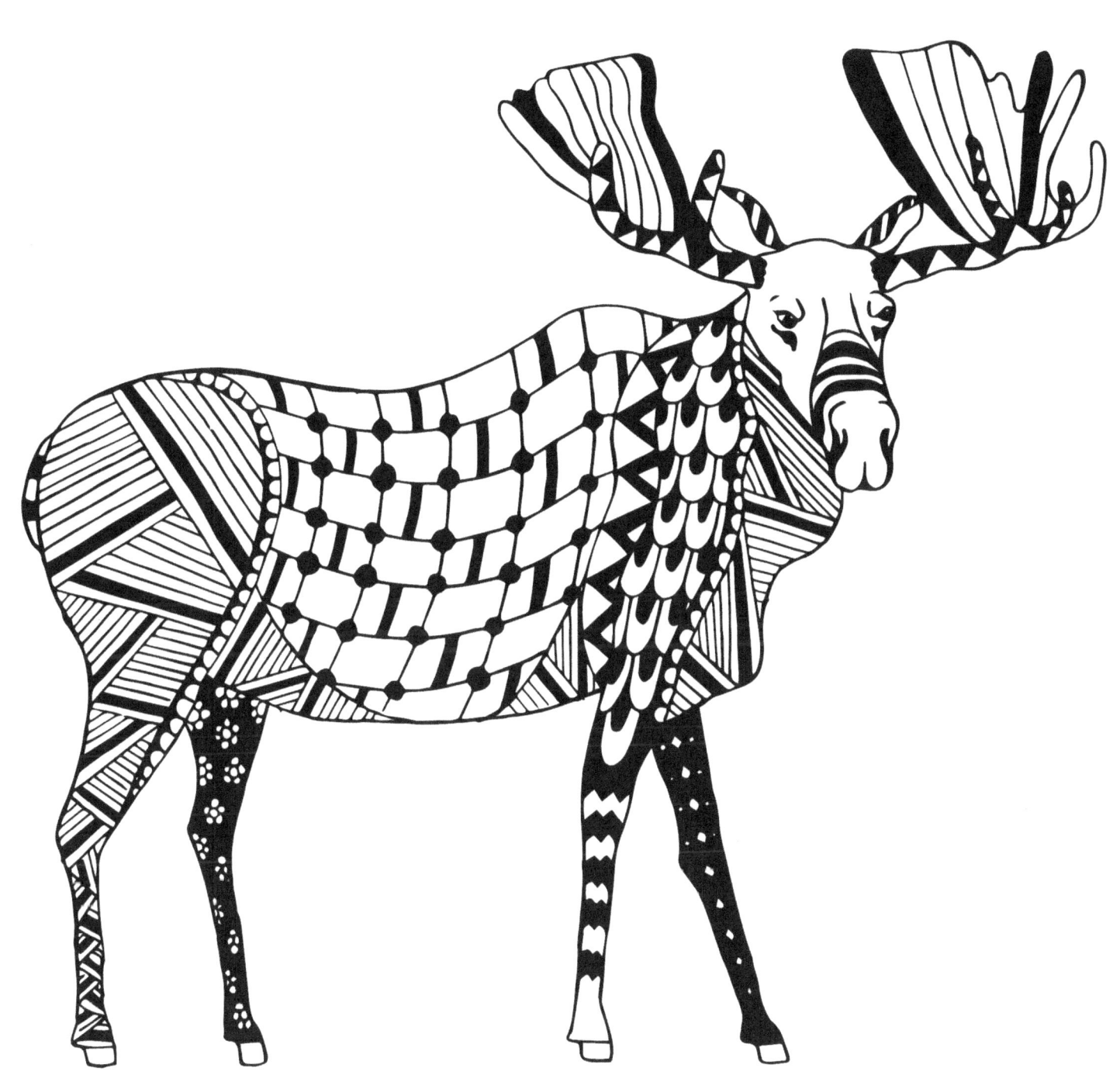

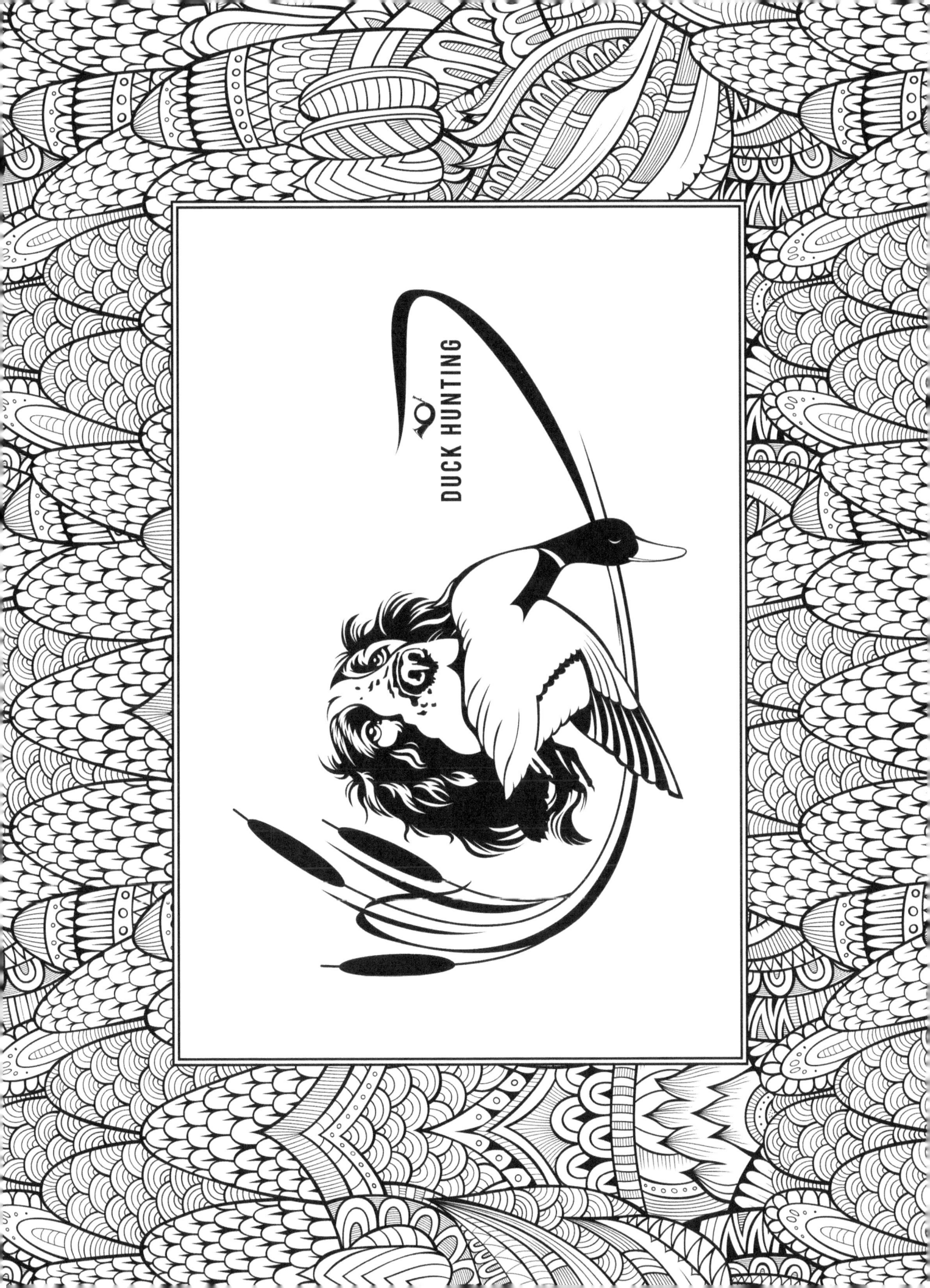

DUCK HUNTING

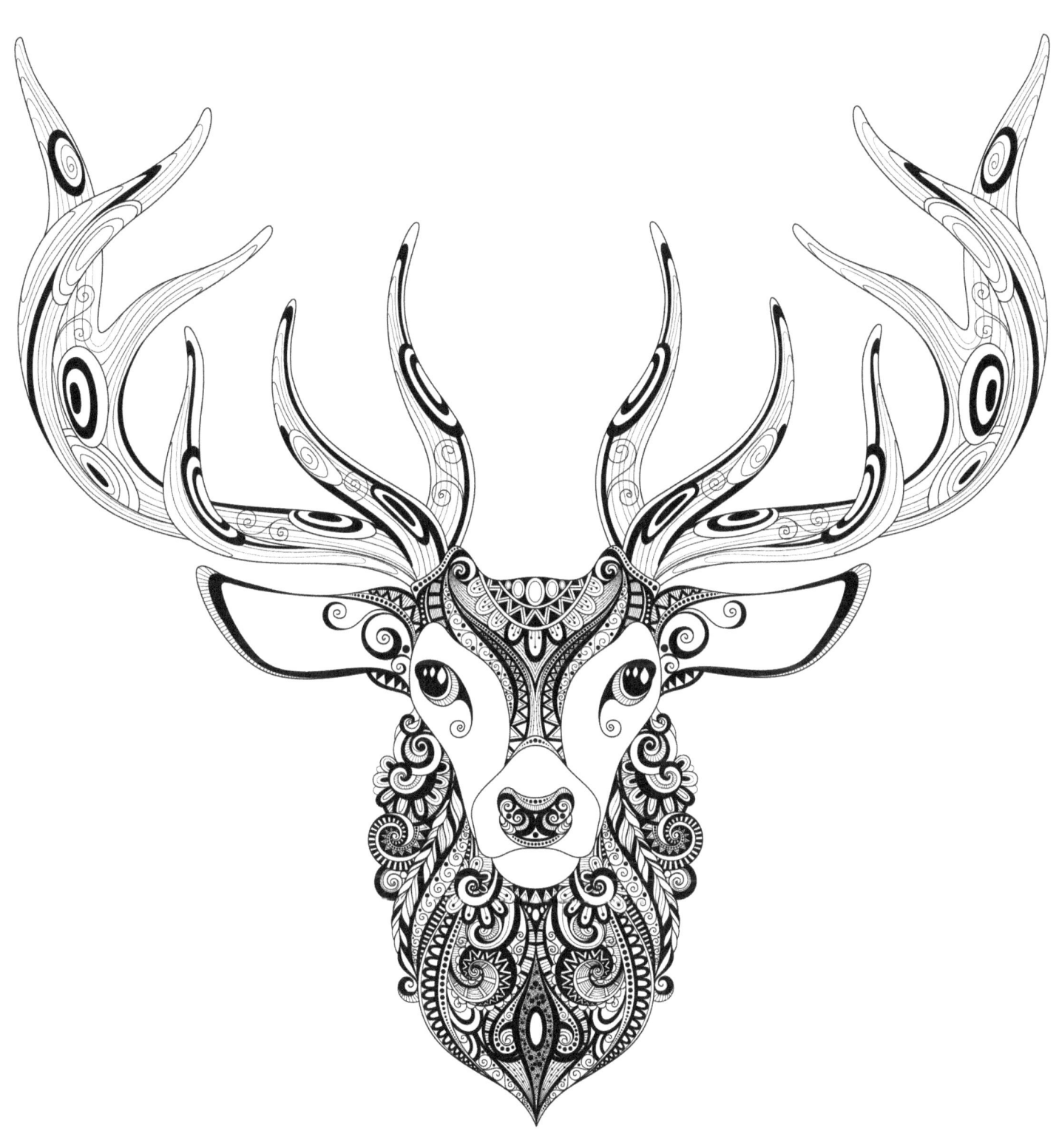

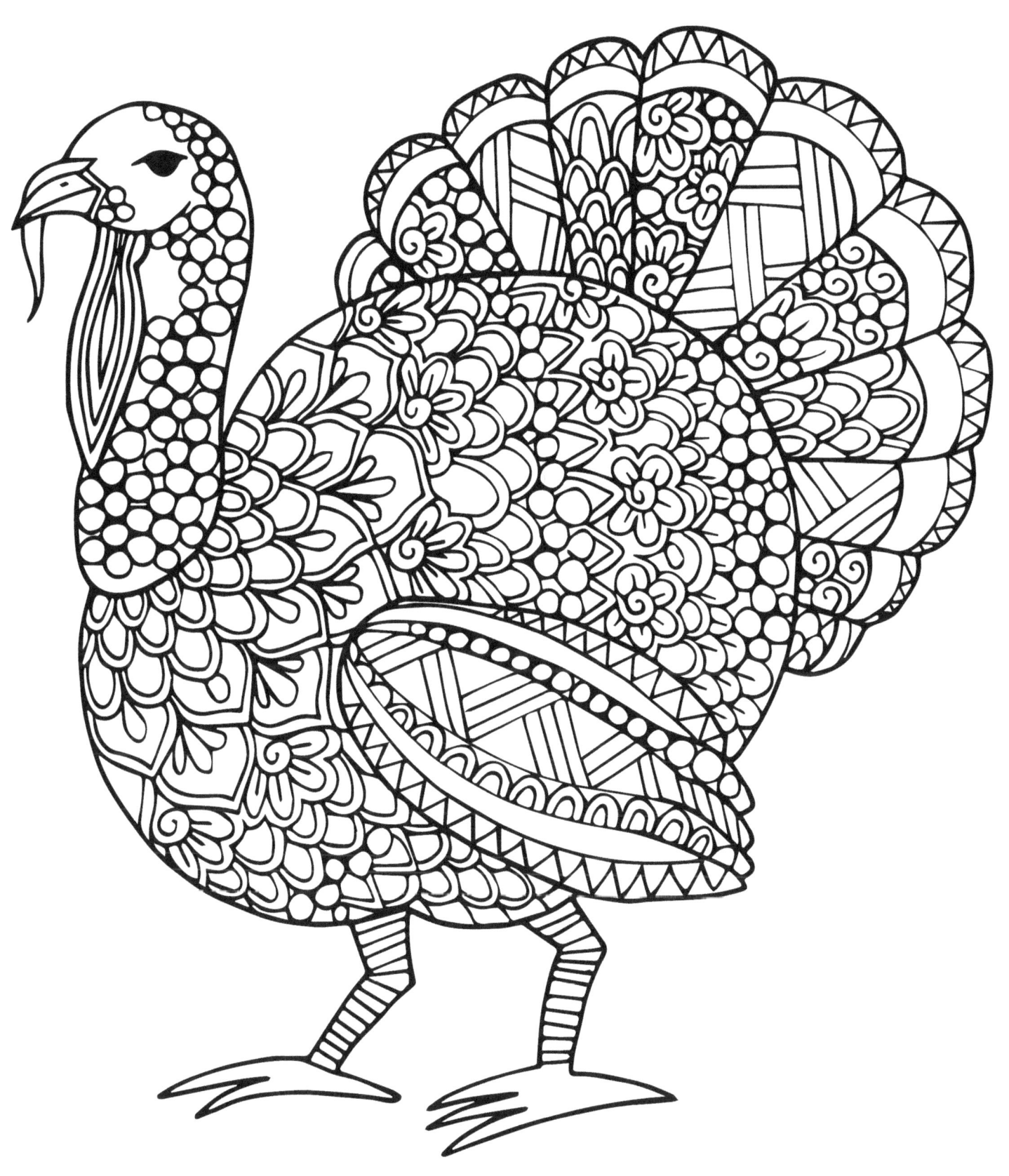

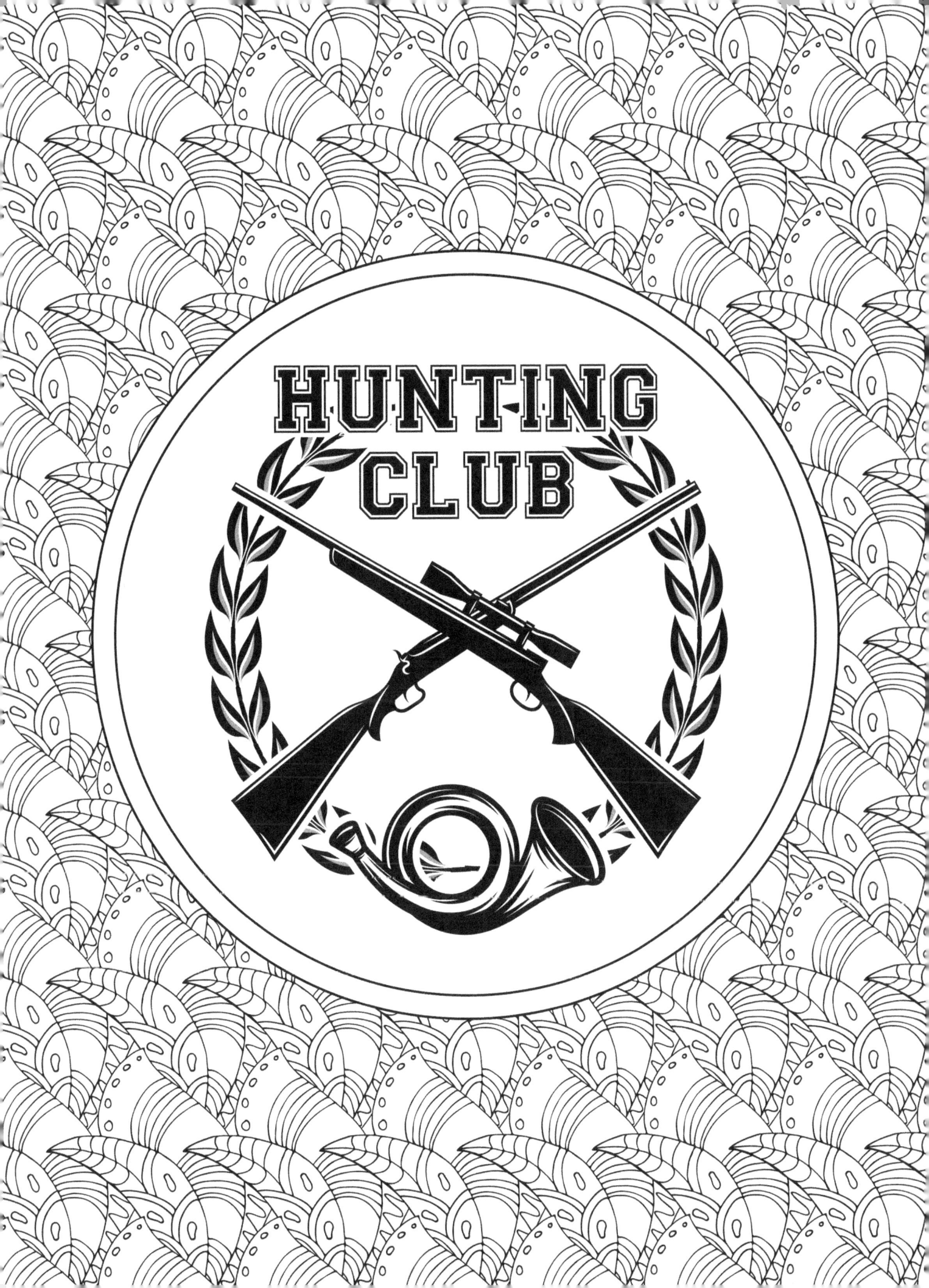

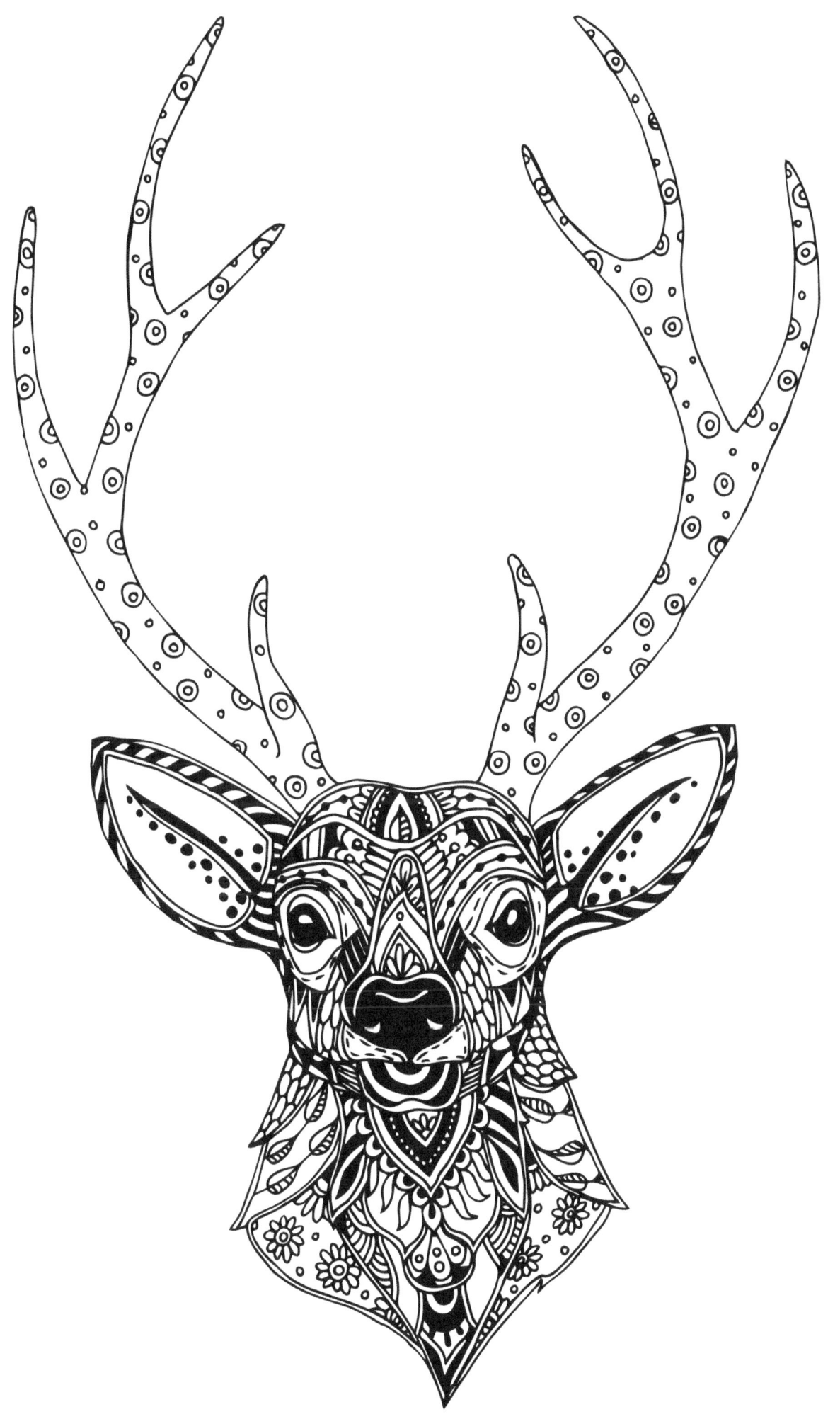

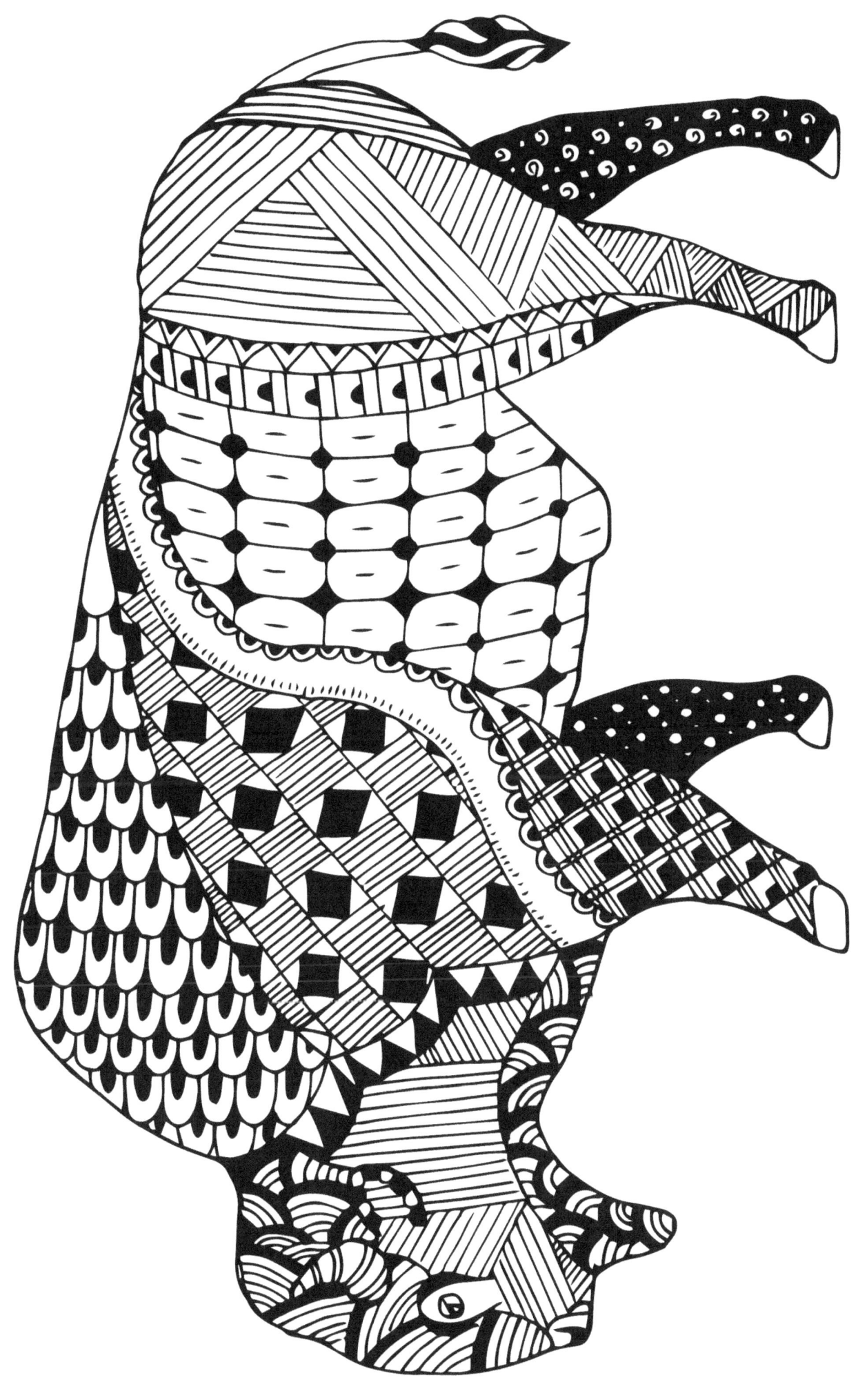

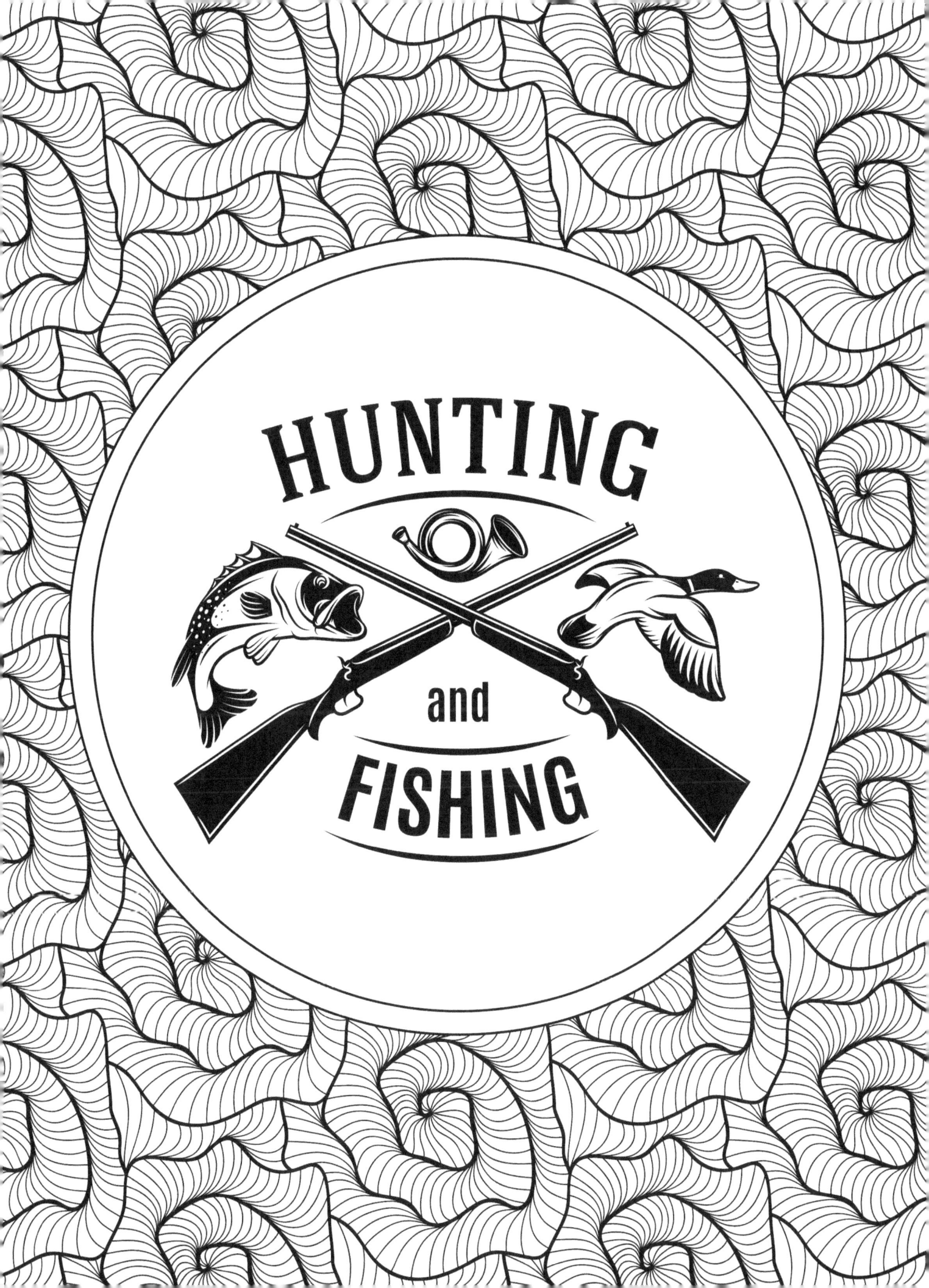

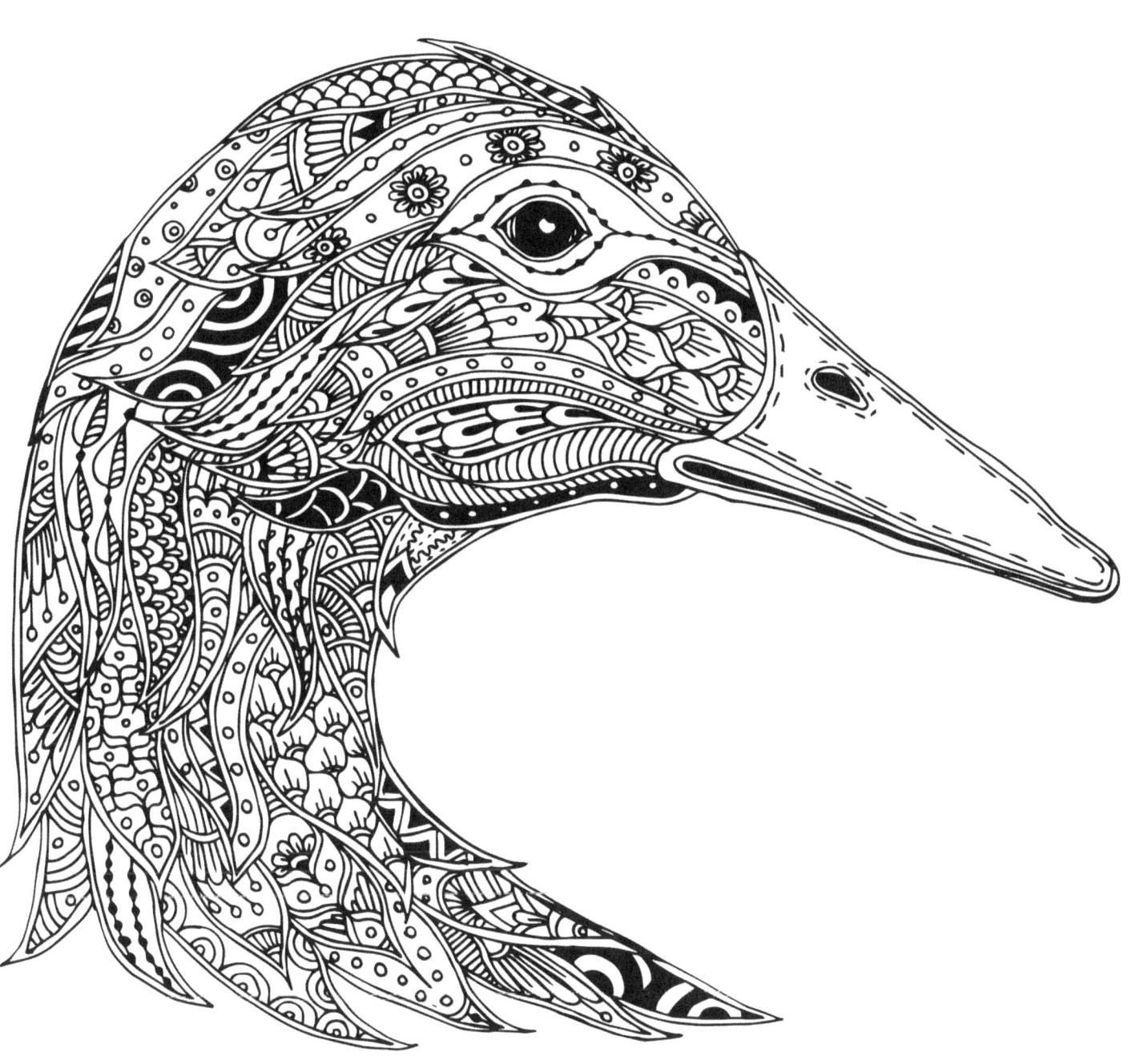

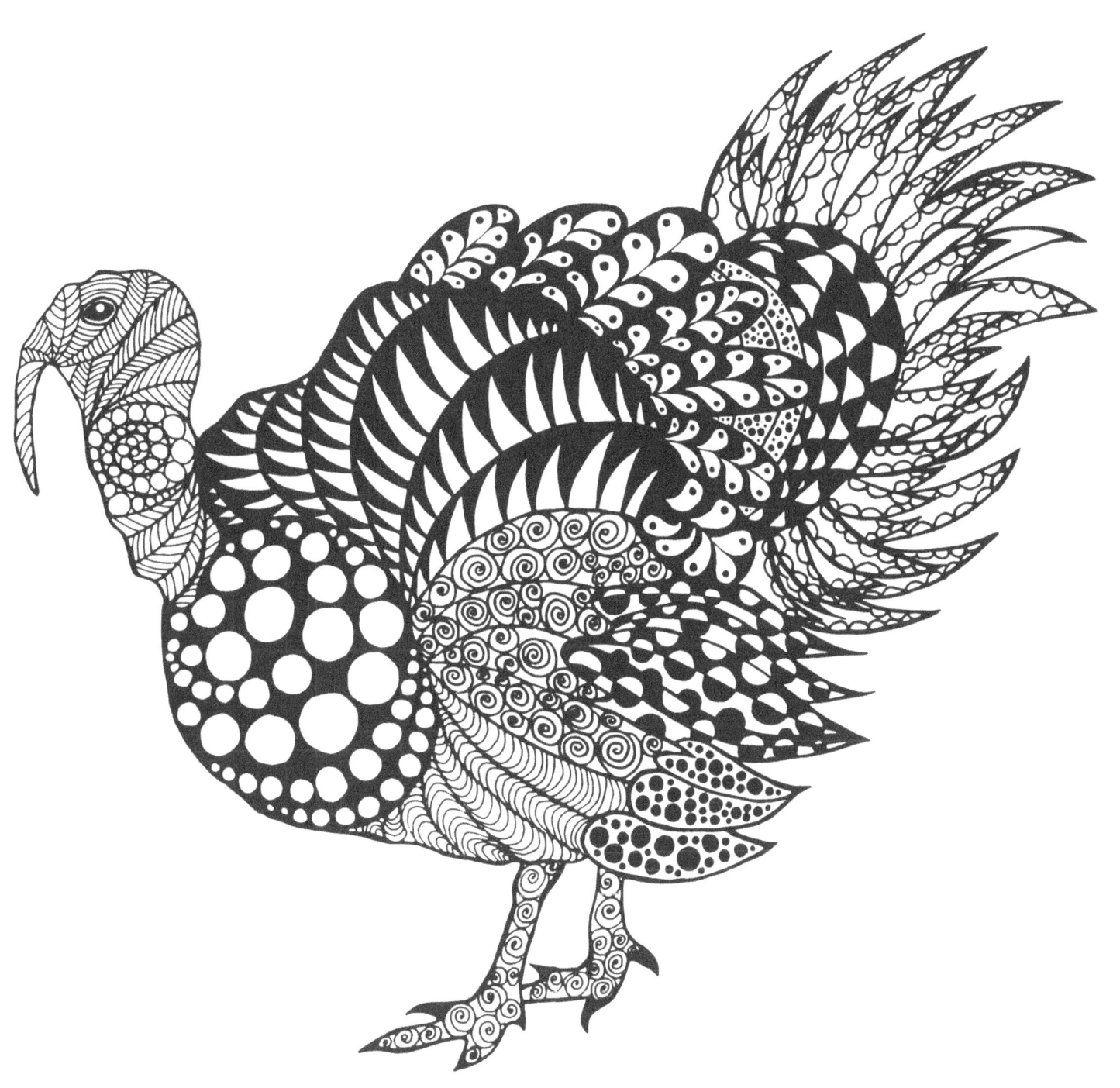

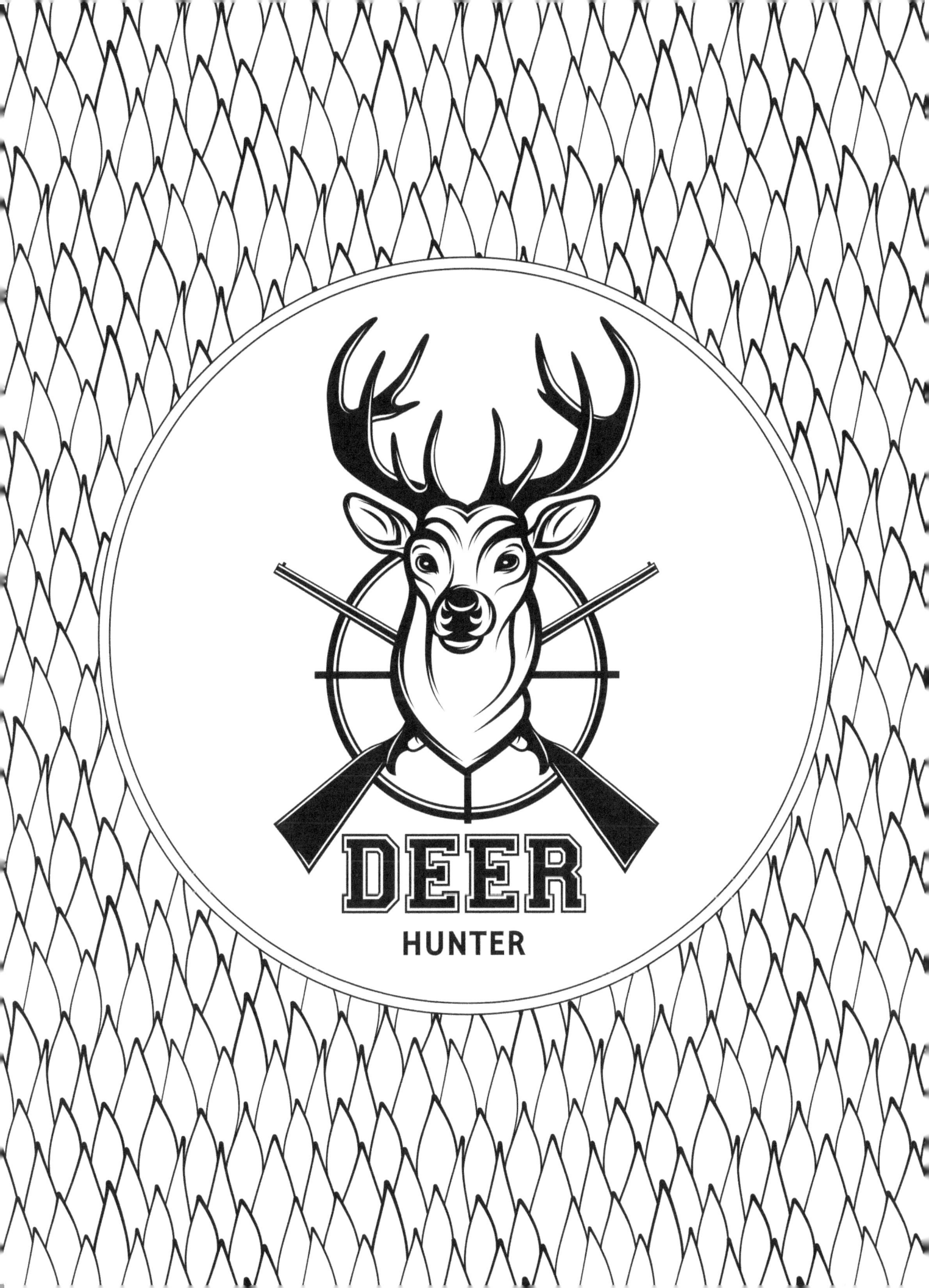

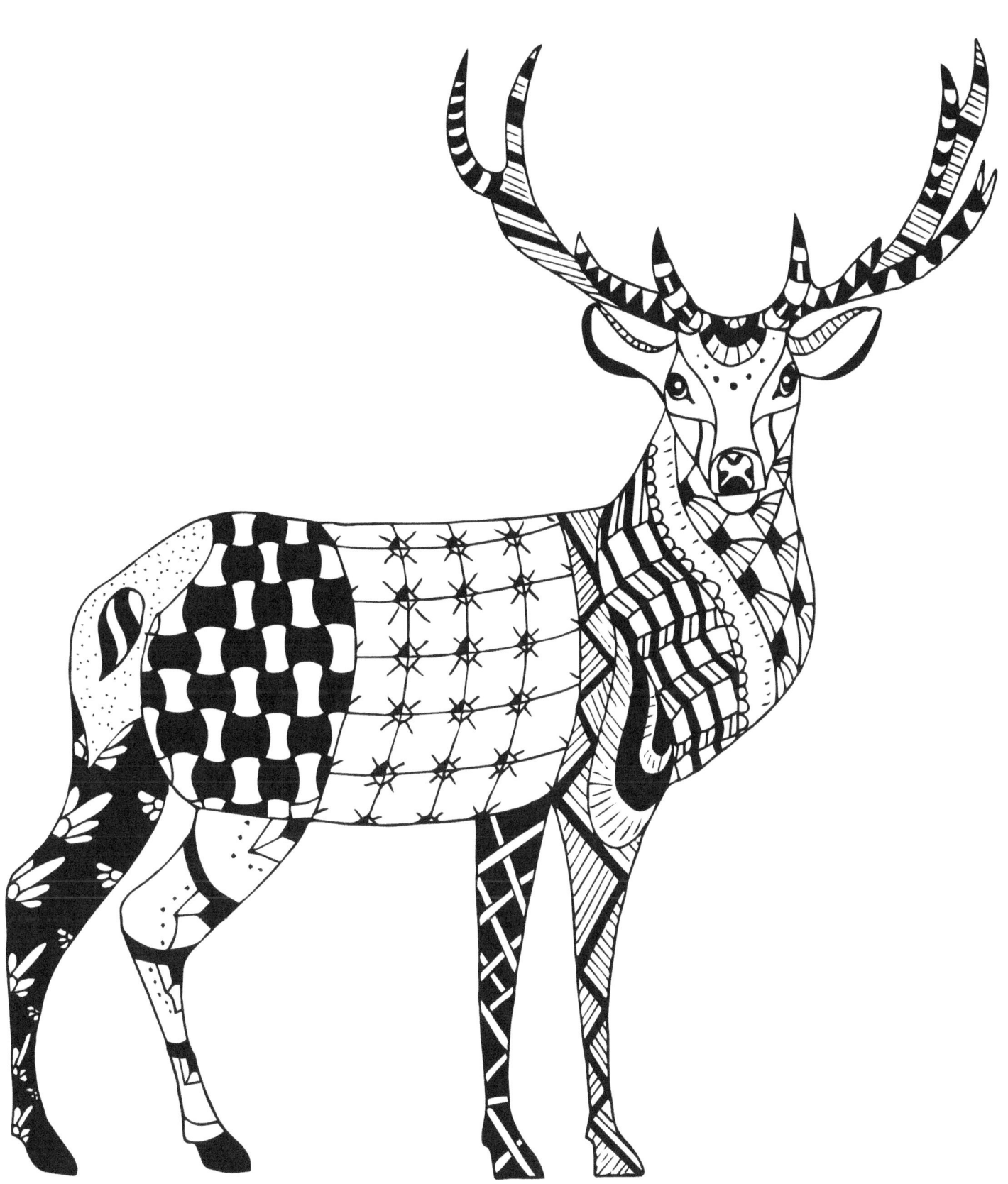

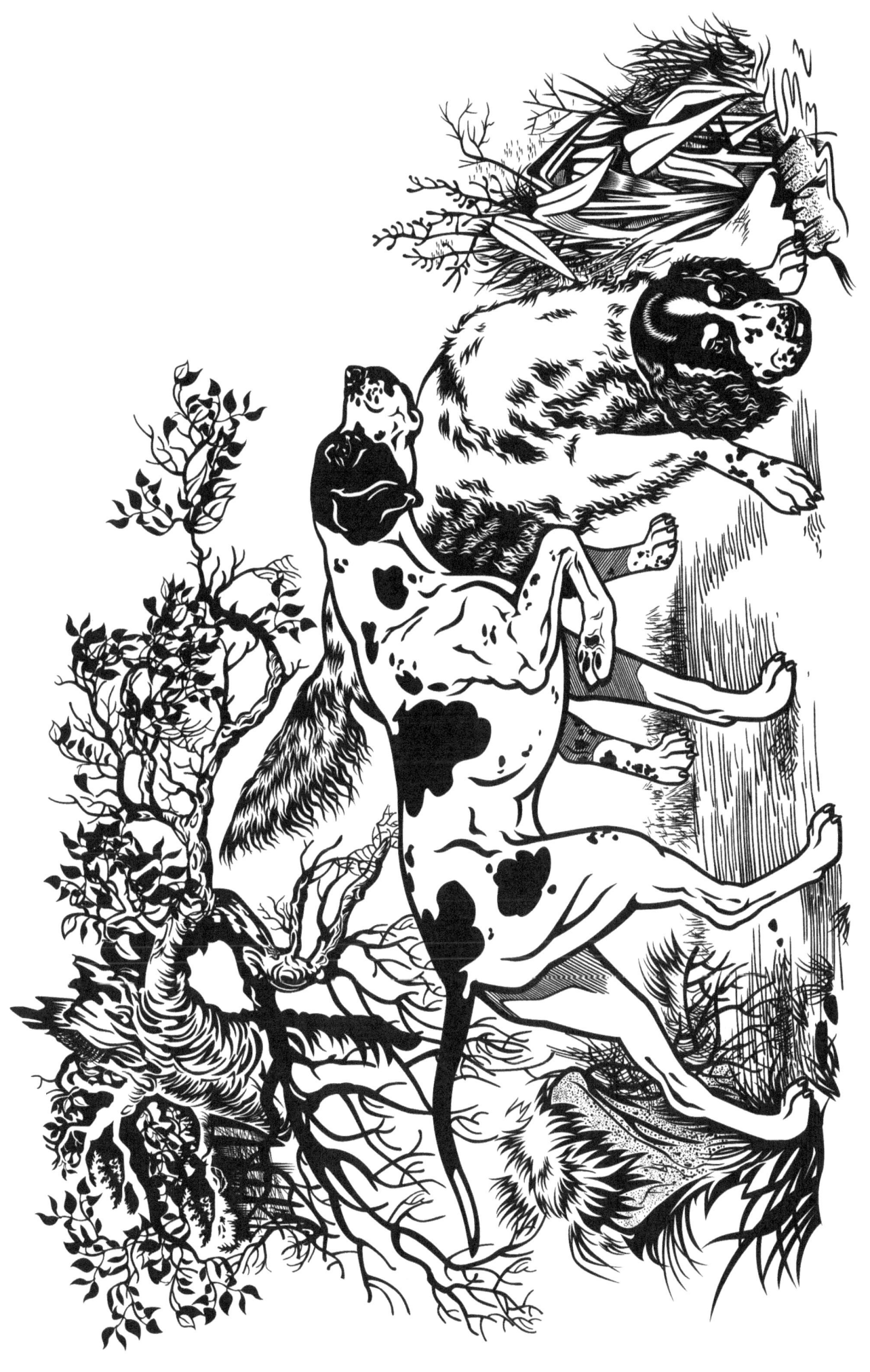

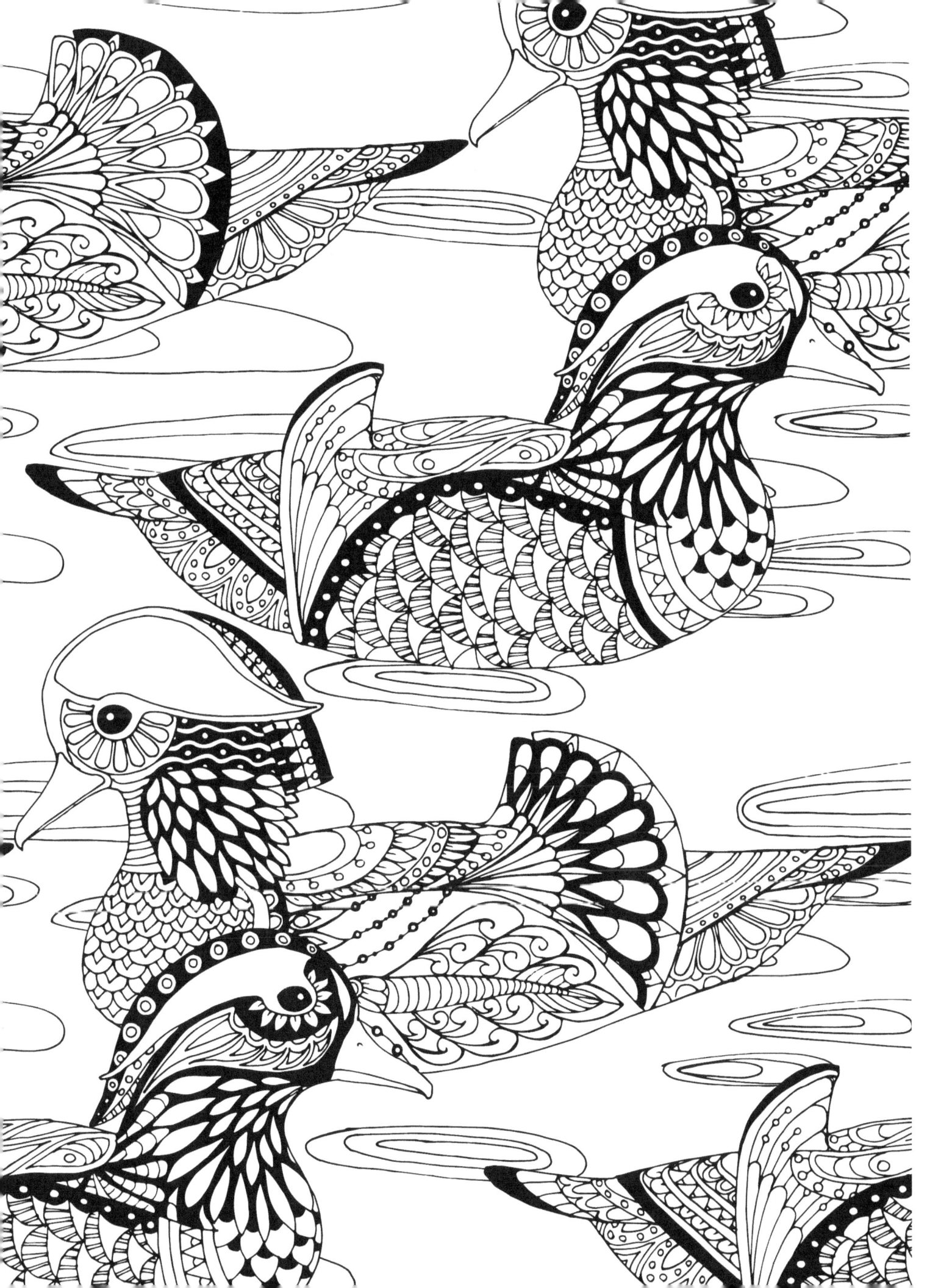

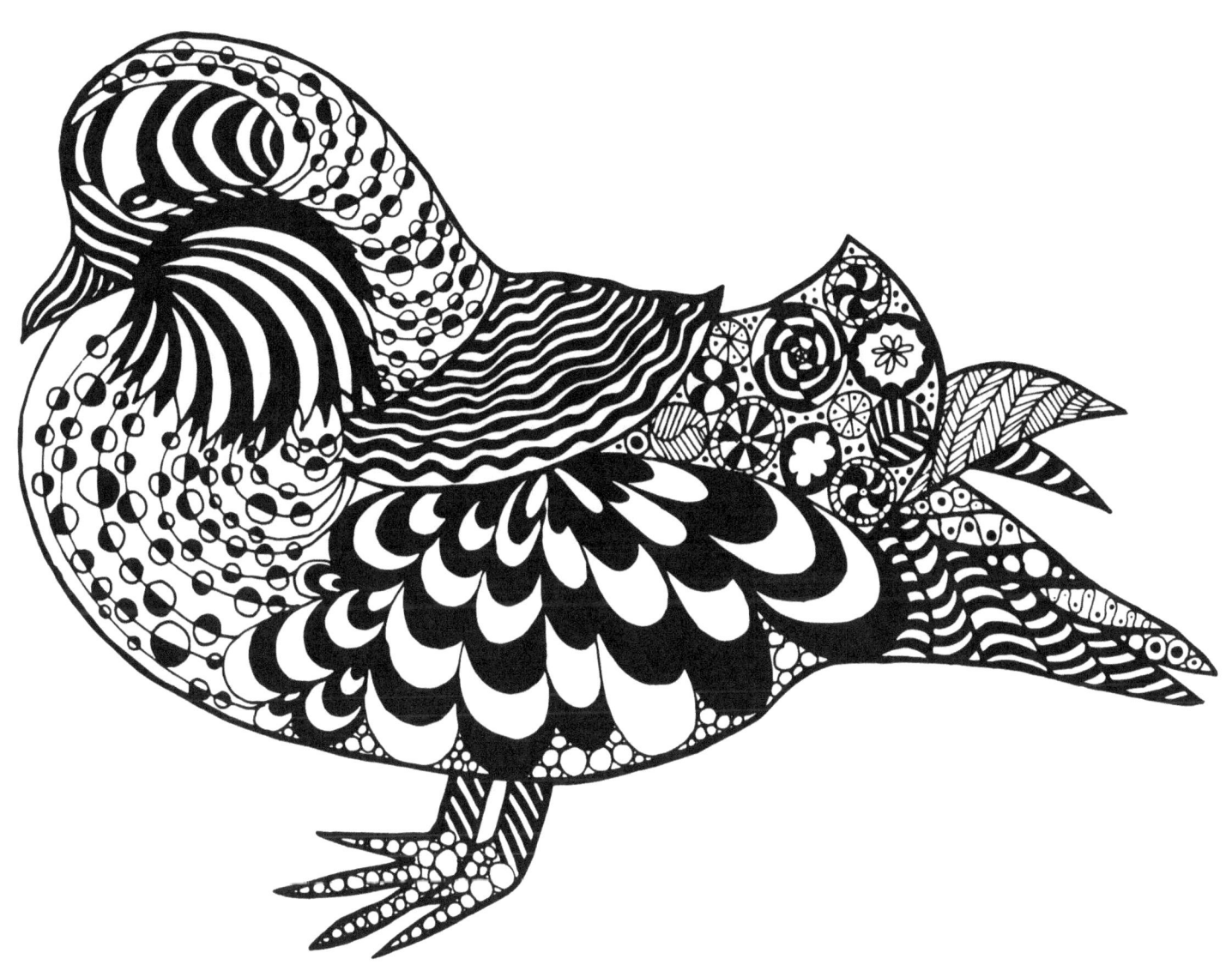

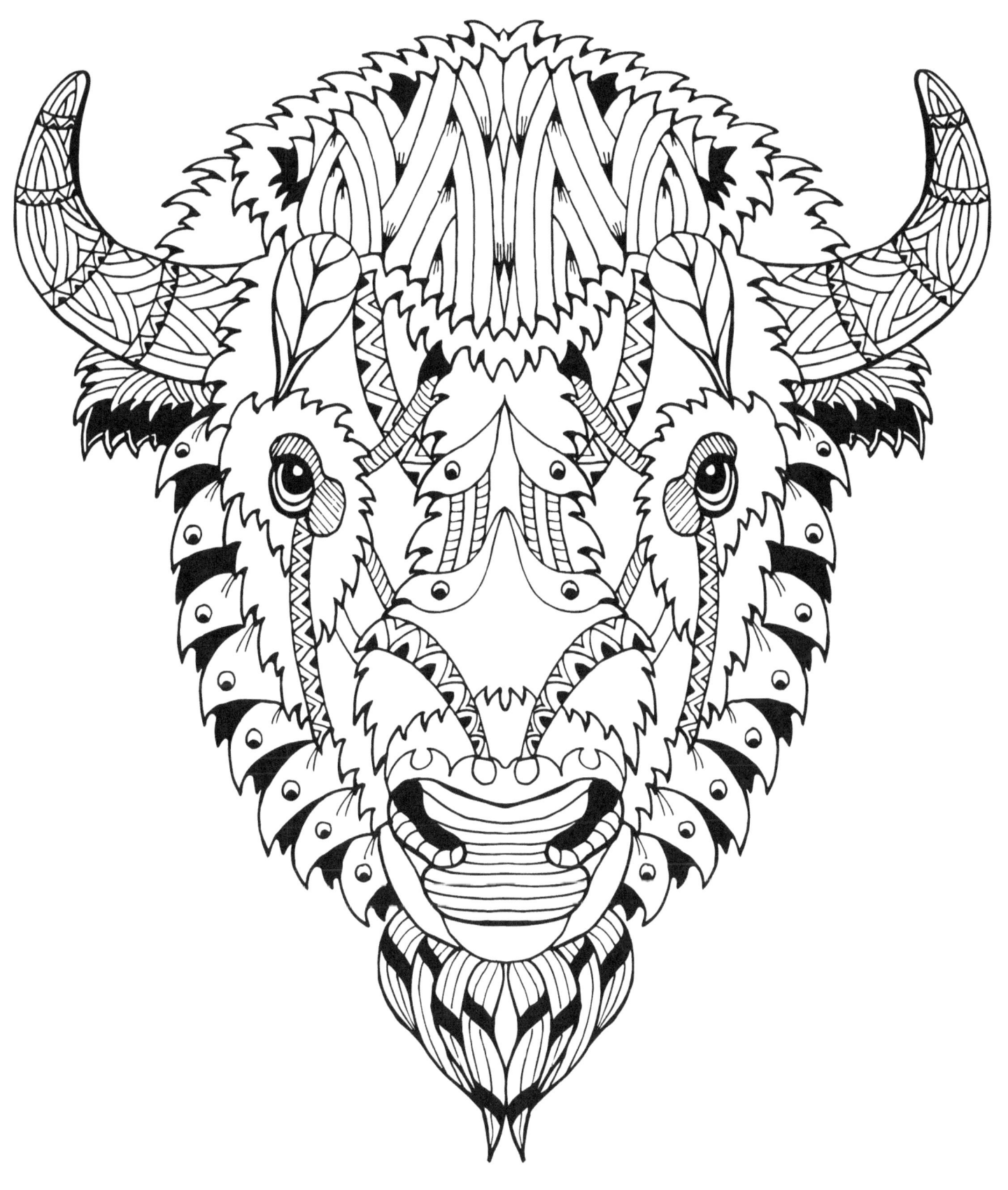

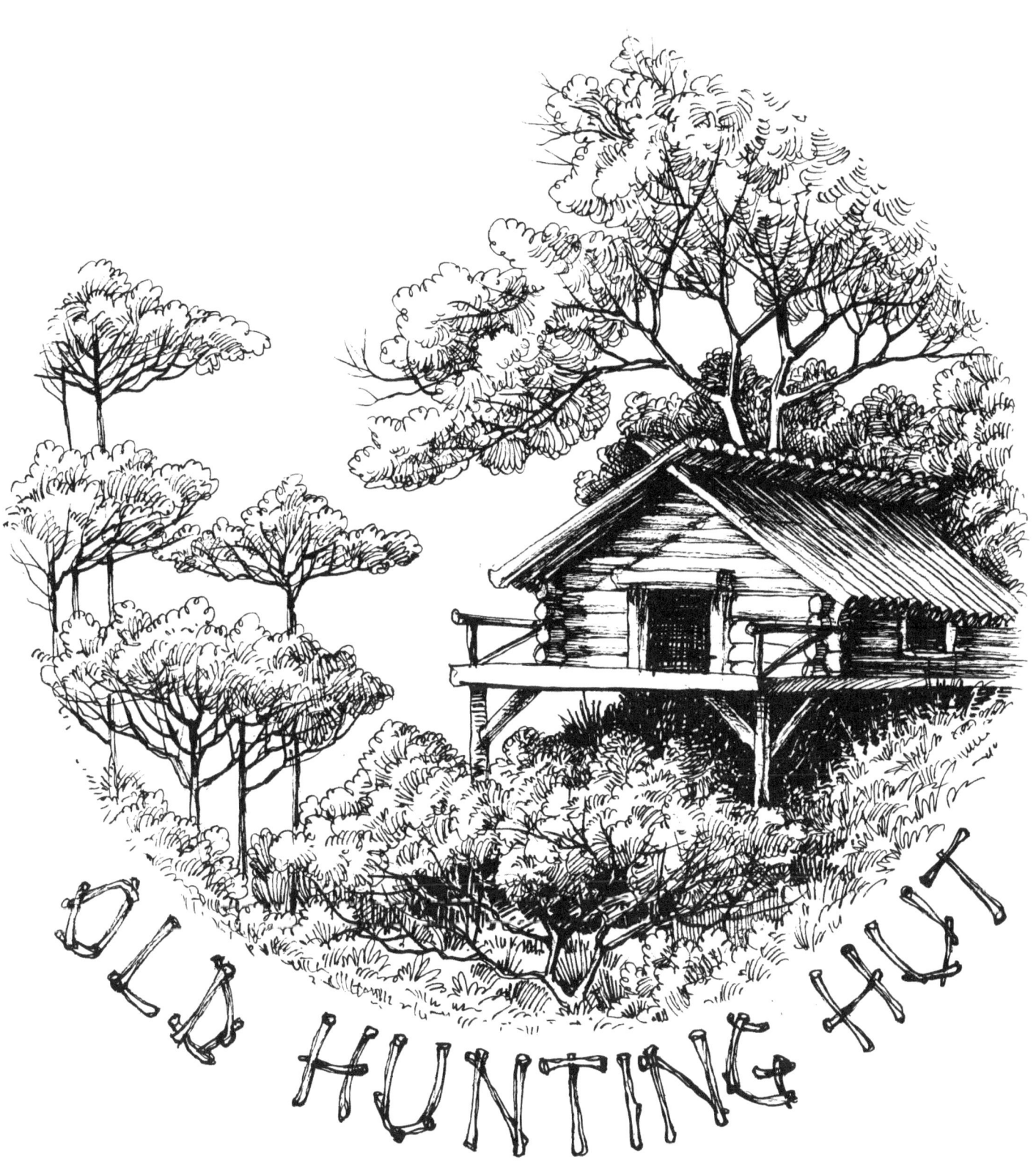

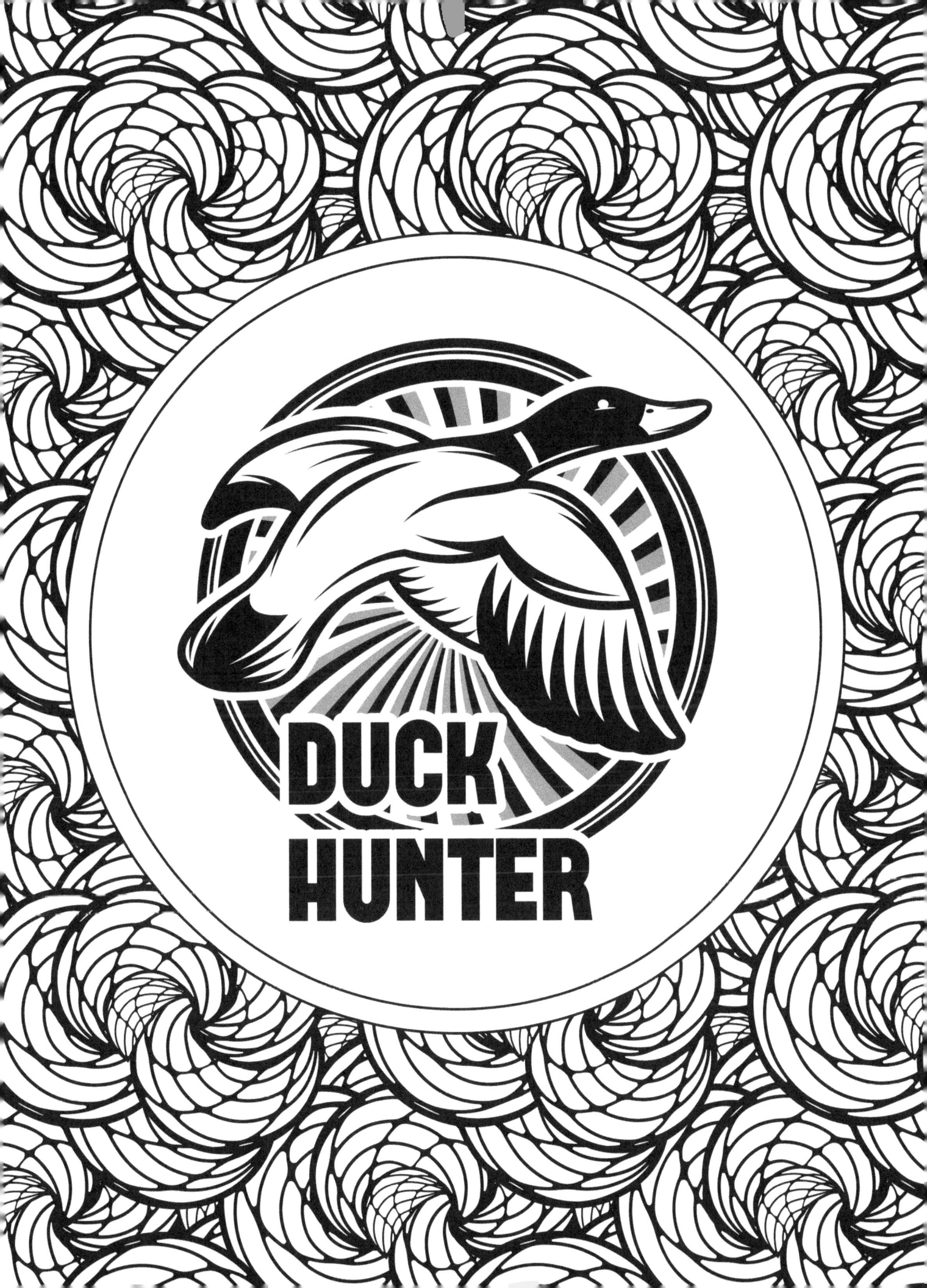

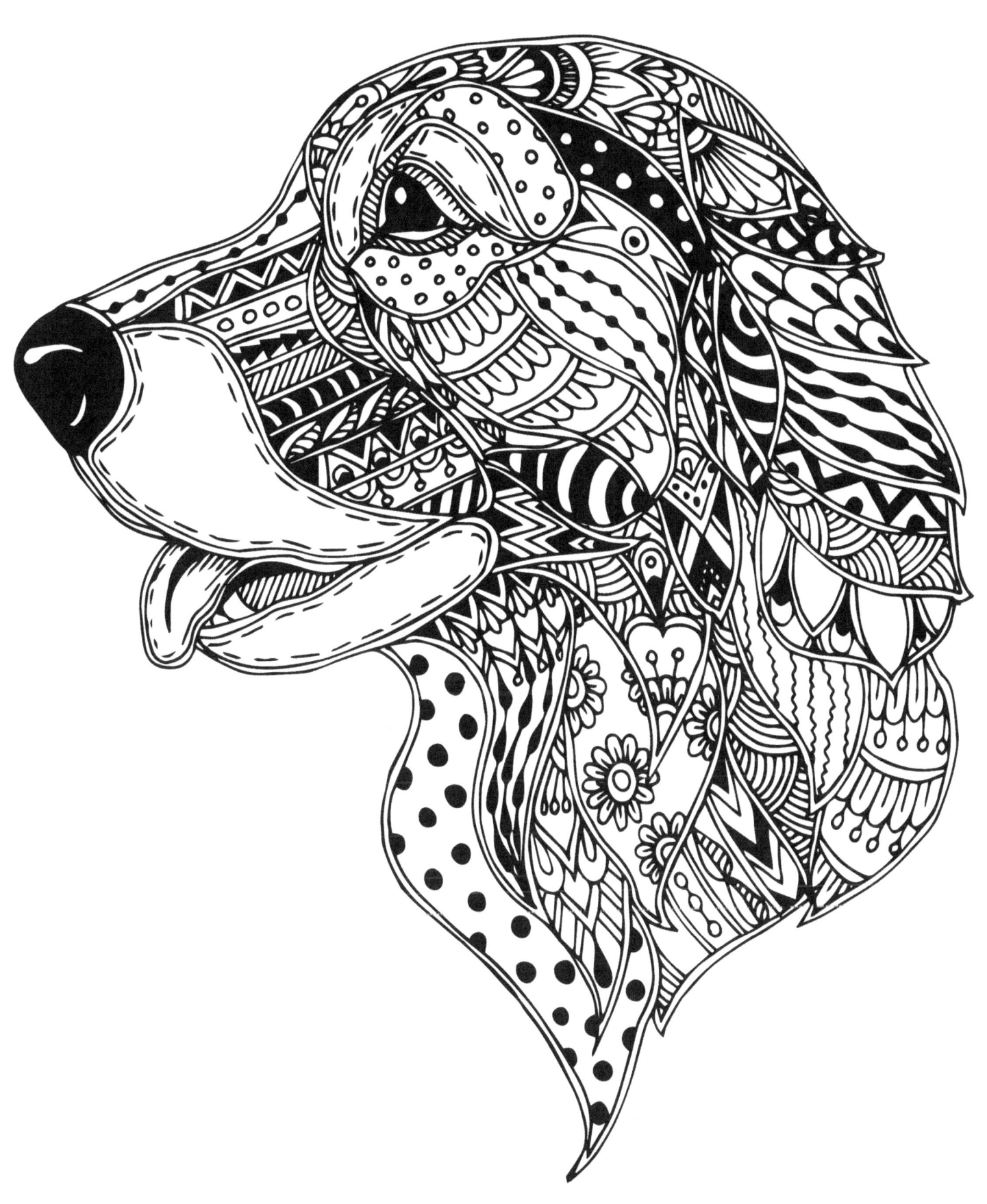

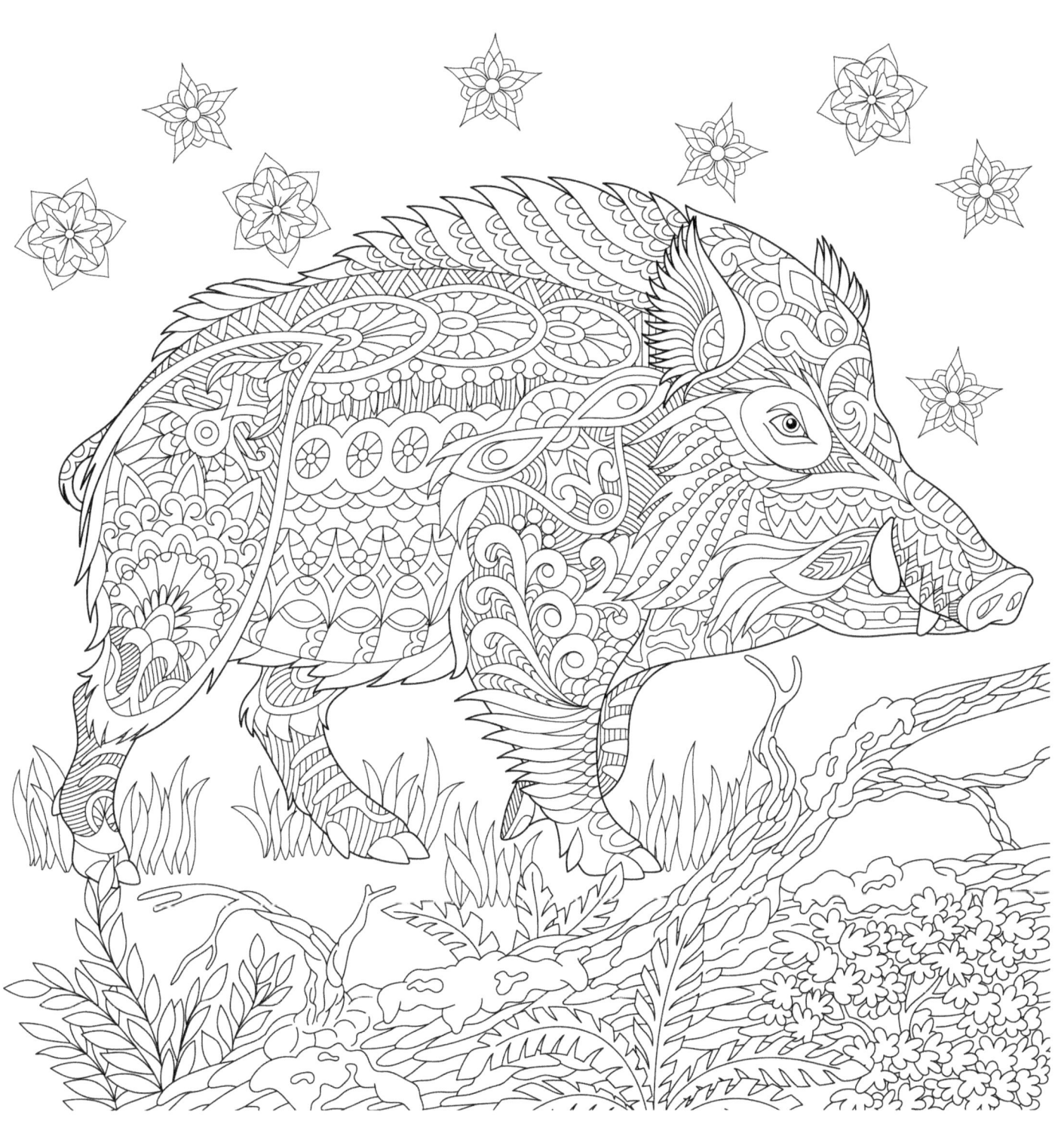

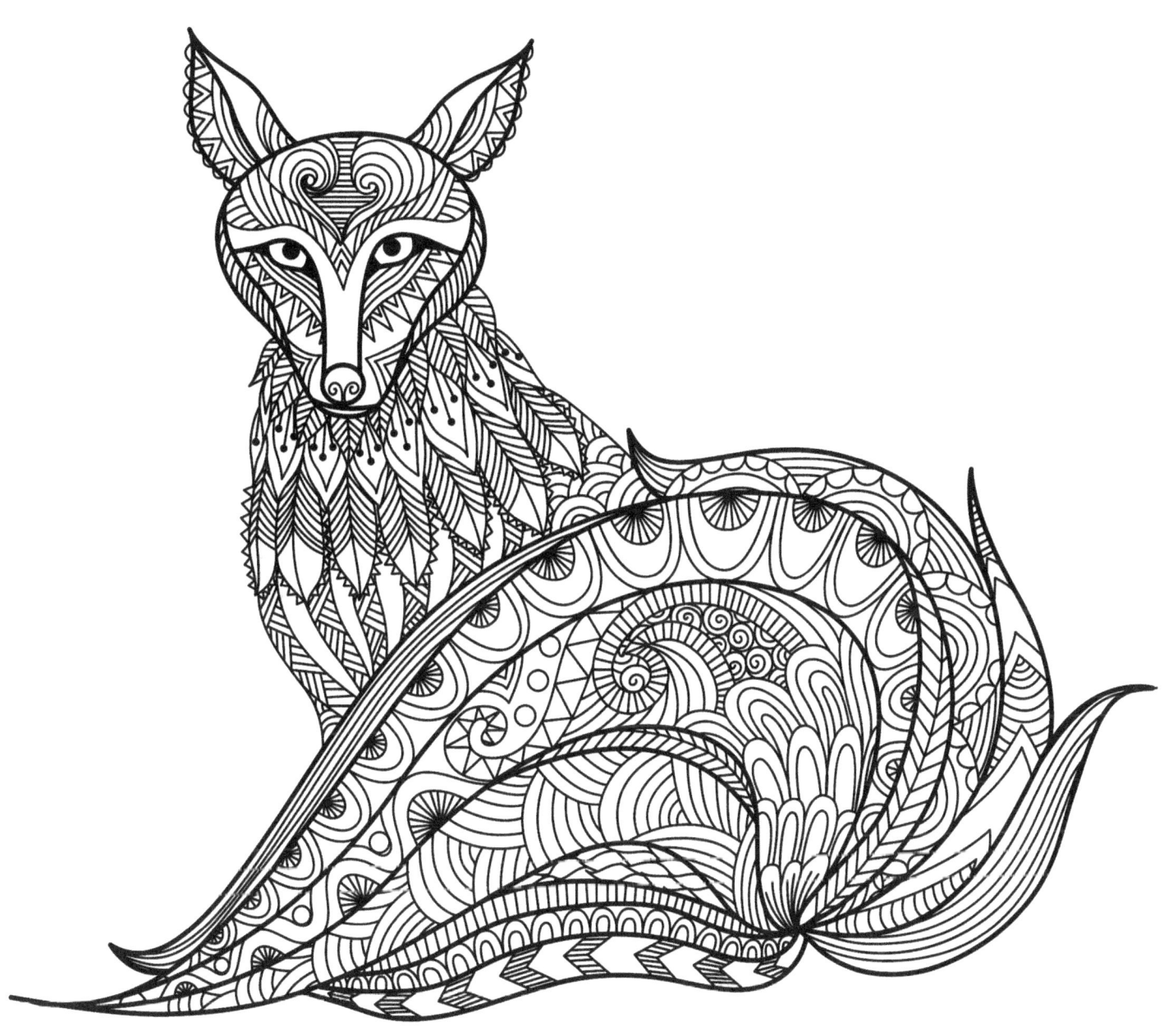

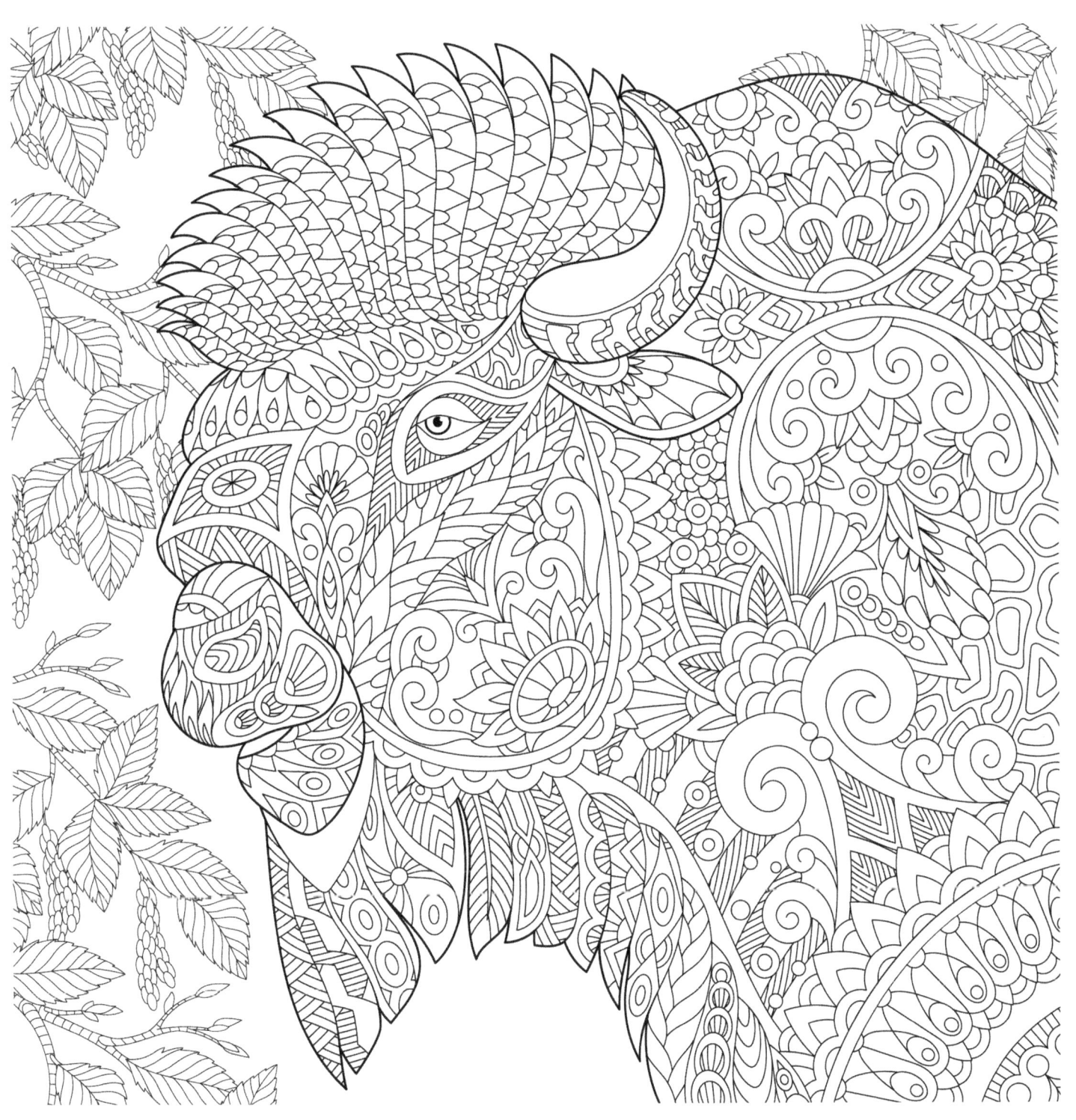

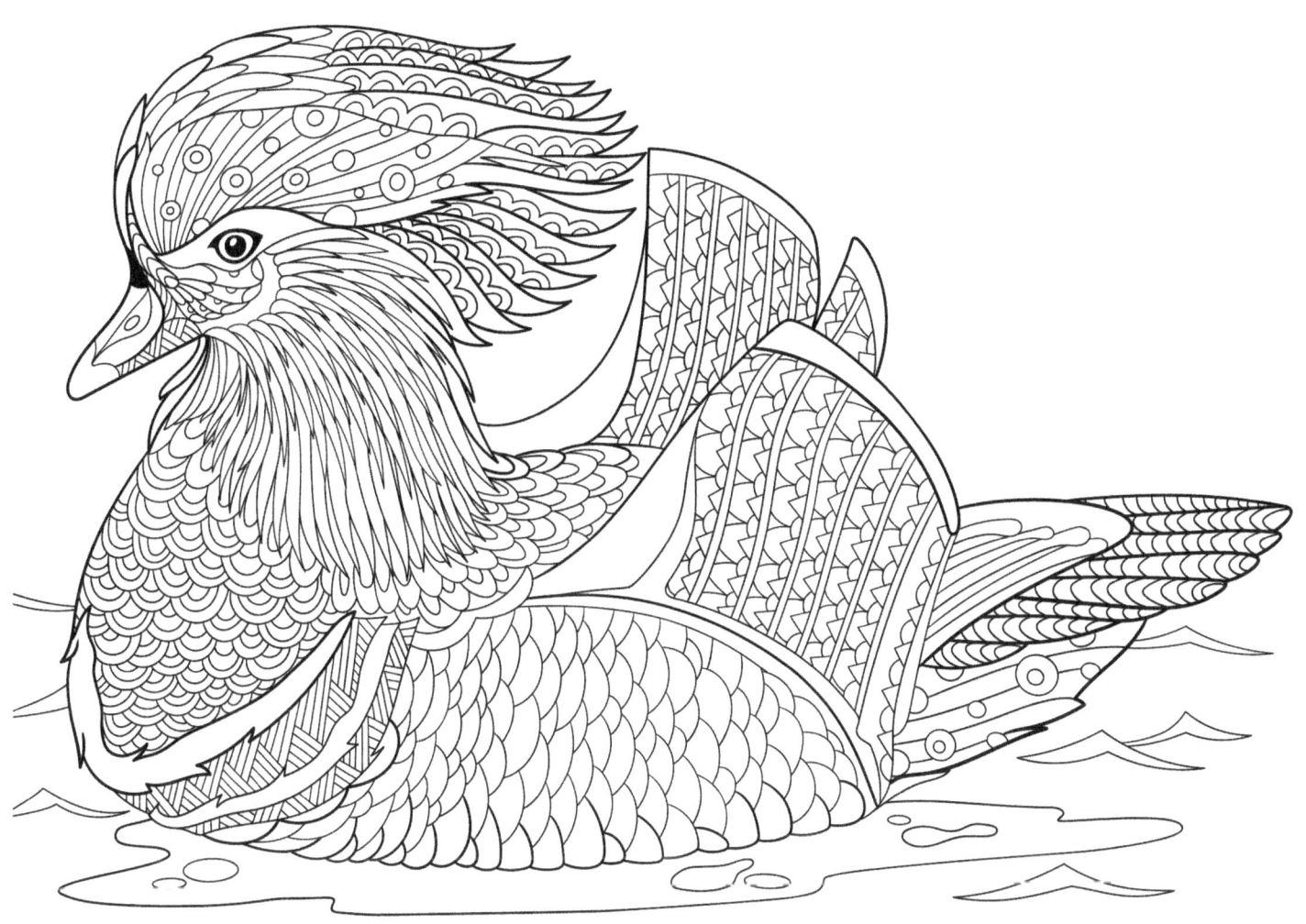

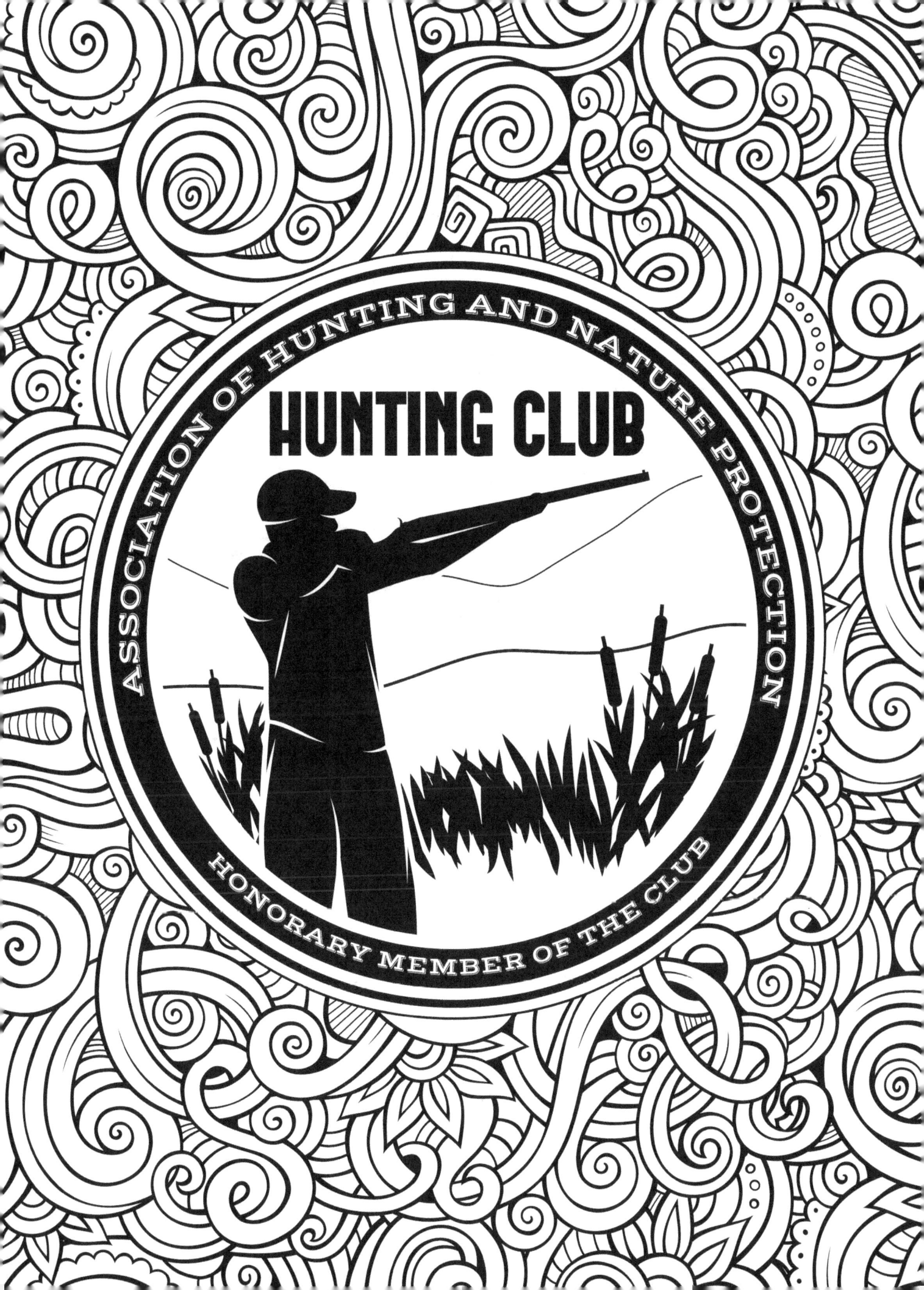

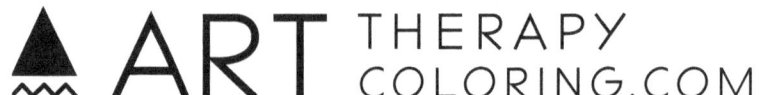

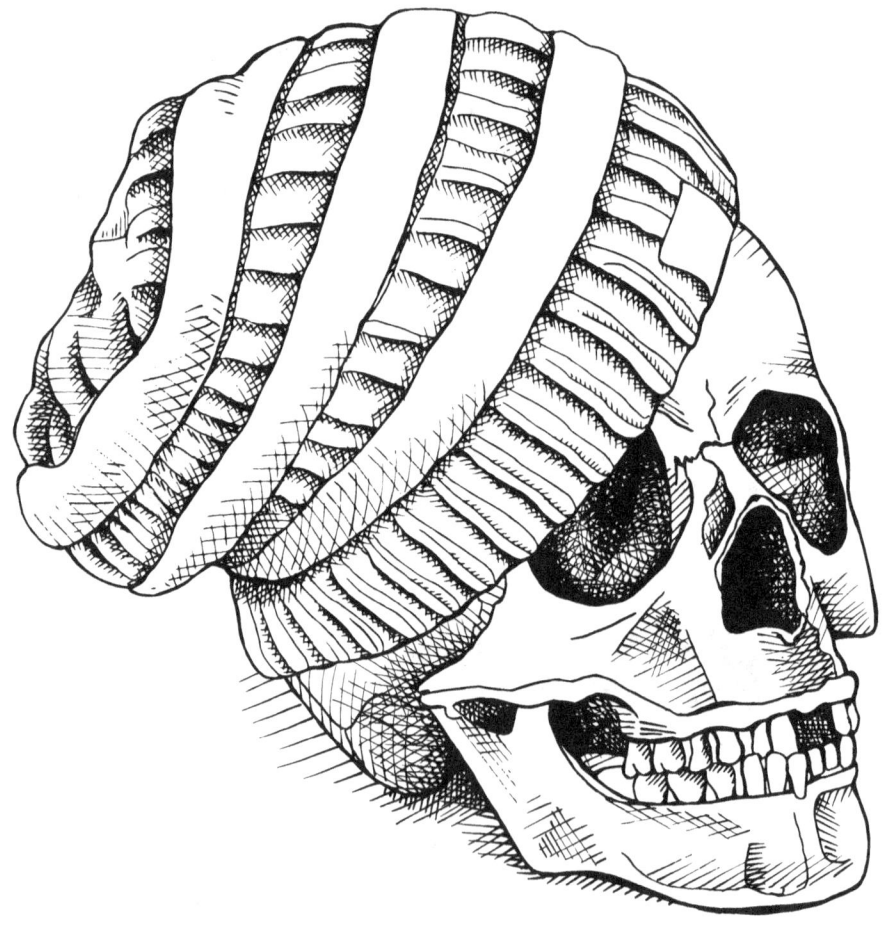

Visit our website at www.arttherapycoloring.com

Get a Free Printable Coloring Ebook!

We've created an exclusive offer for our customers to receive a free Adult Coloring Ebook.

Visit **www.arttherapycoloring.com/freebie** to claim your free coloring book with over 30 new designs that you can instantly print and color!

Over 100 Art Therapy Coloring Books

See our collection of over 100 Art Therapy Coloring Books for Adults, Men, Seniors, Teens, Kids, Boys, and Girls on the following pages.

Coloring Books For Men

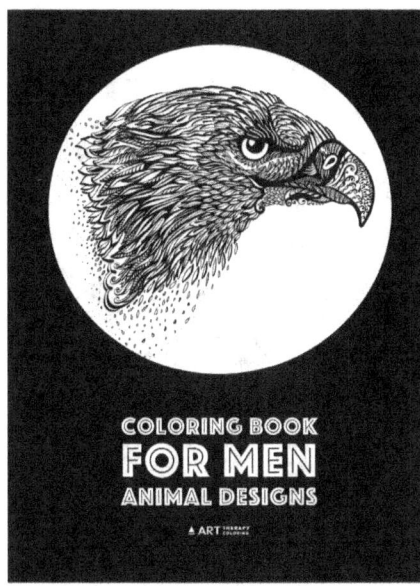

COLORING BOOK
FOR MEN
ANIMAL DESIGNS
ART THERAPY COLORING

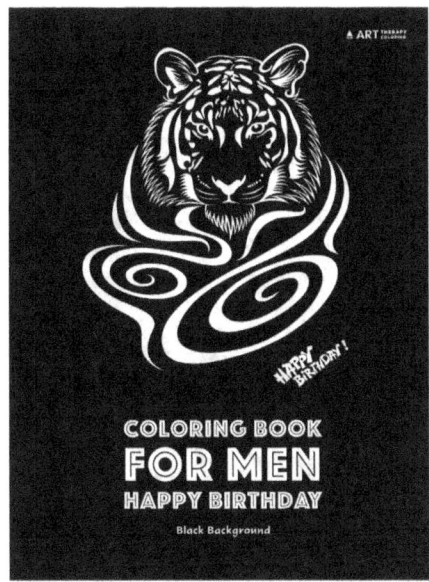

COLORING BOOK
FOR MEN
HAPPY BIRTHDAY
Black Background

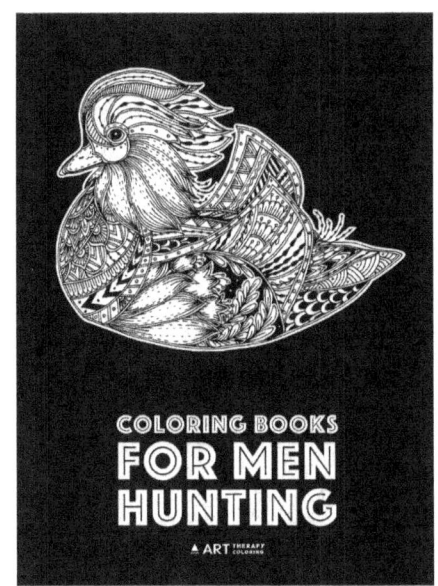

COLORING BOOKS
FOR MEN
HUNTING
ART THERAPY COLORING

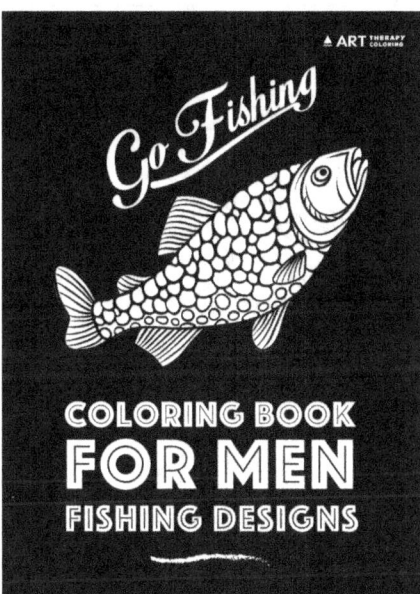

COLORING BOOK
FOR MEN
FISHING DESIGNS

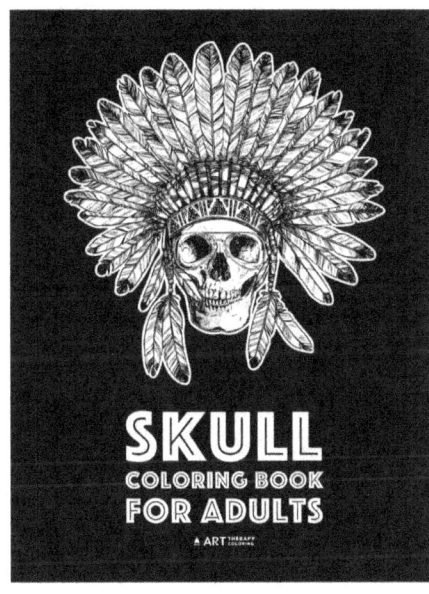

SKULL
COLORING BOOK
FOR ADULTS
ART THERAPY COLORING

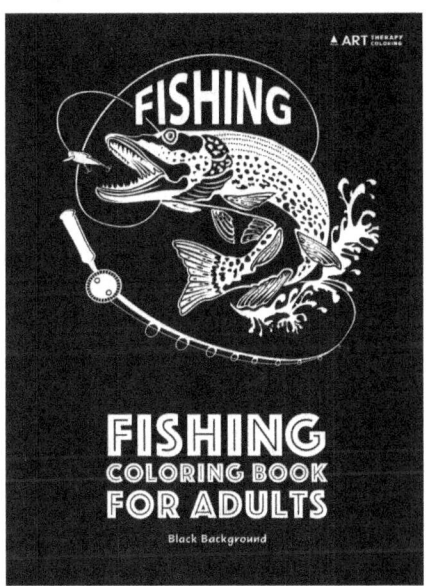

FISHING
COLORING BOOK
FOR ADULTS
Black Background

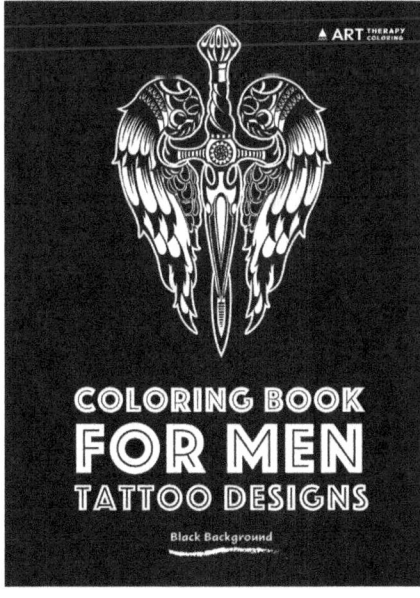

COLORING BOOK
FOR MEN
TATTOO DESIGNS
Black Background

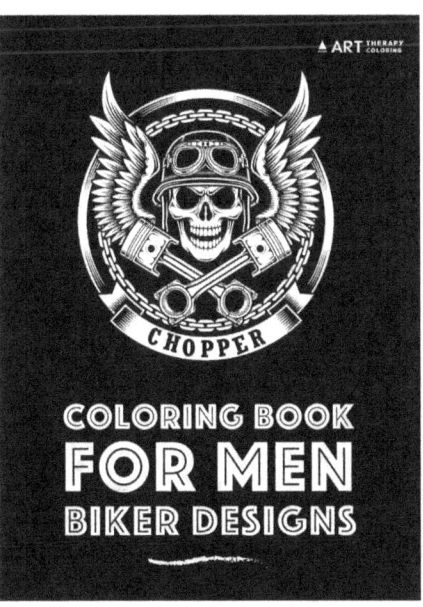

COLORING BOOK
FOR MEN
BIKER DESIGNS

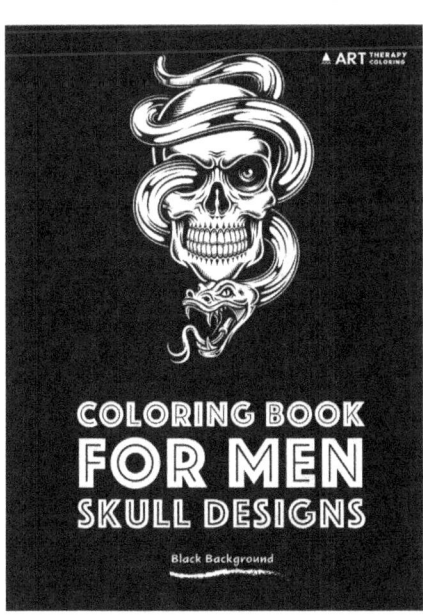

COLORING BOOK
FOR MEN
SKULL DESIGNS
Black Background

Coloring Books For Adults

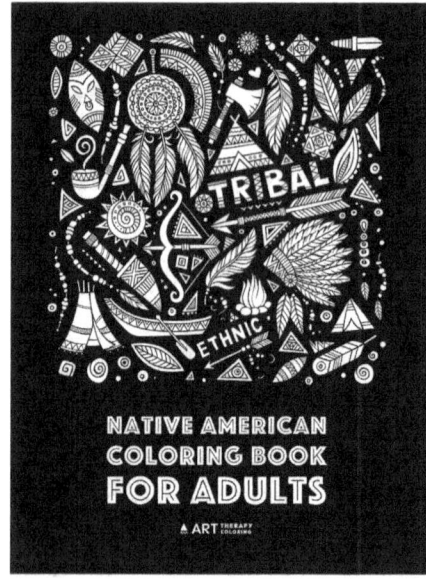

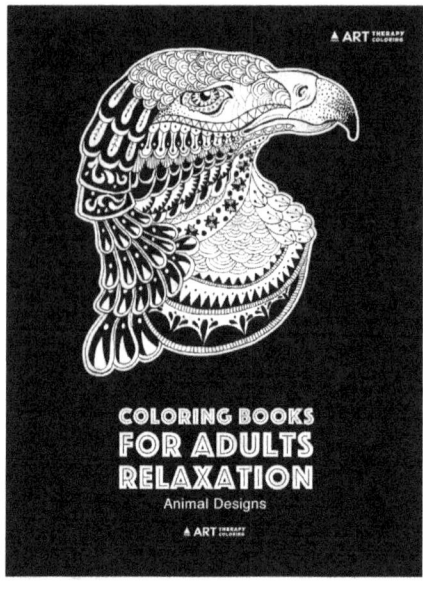

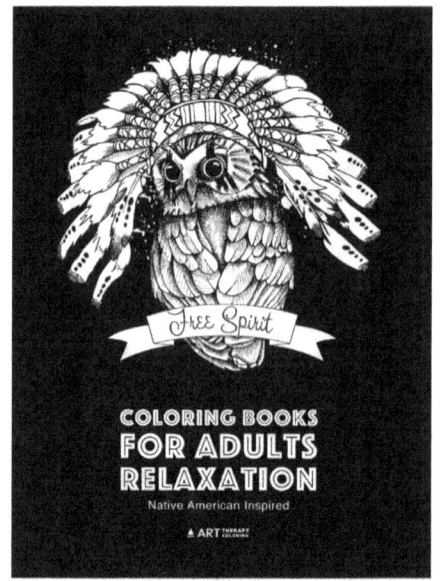

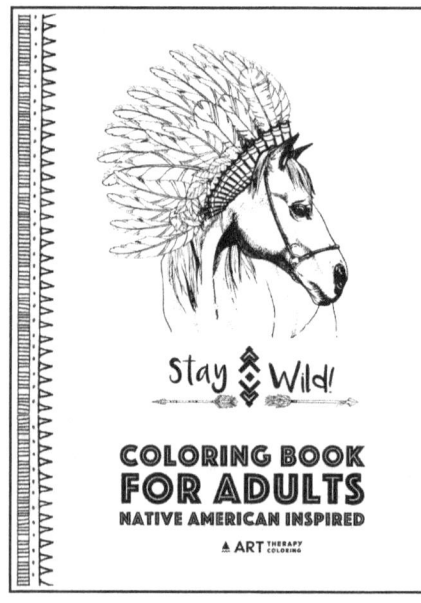

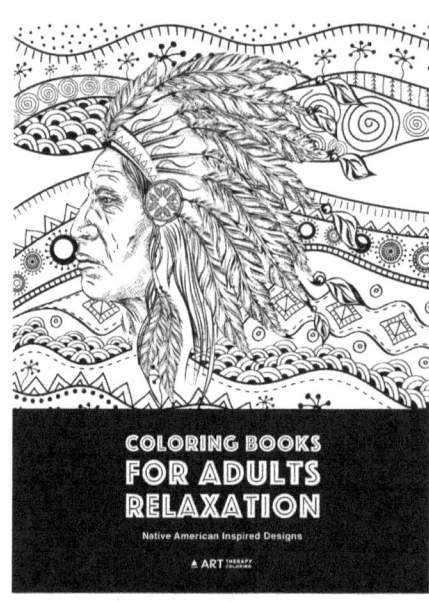

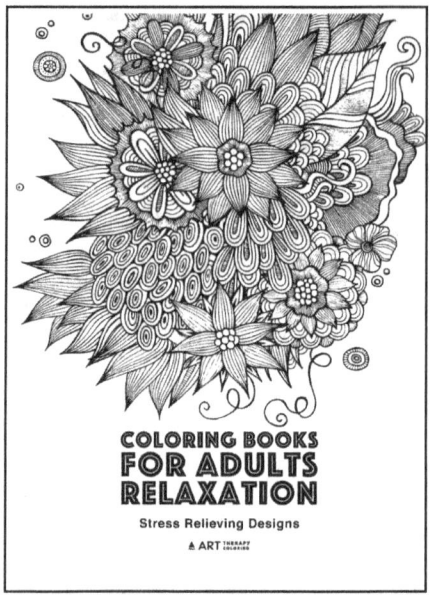

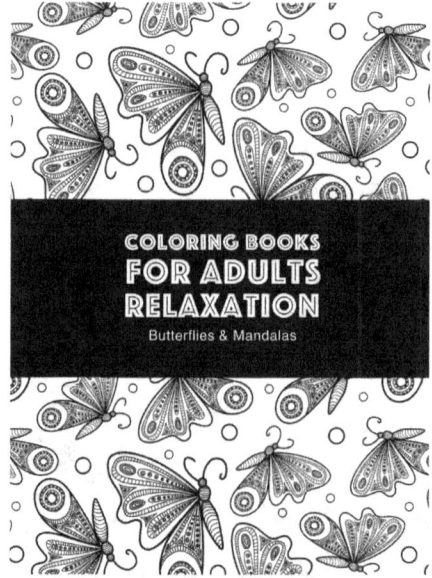

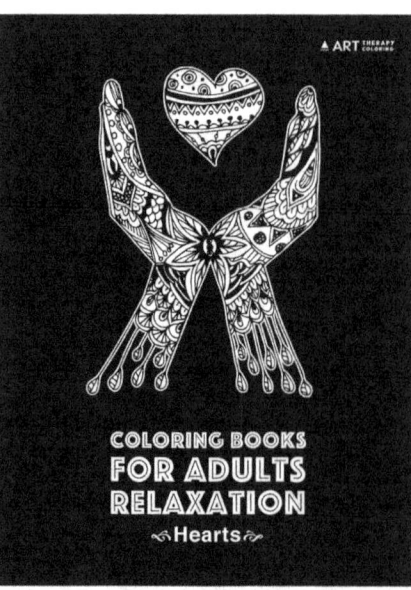

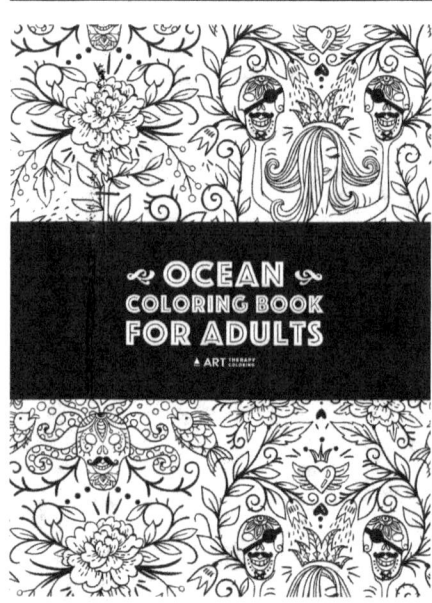

Coloring Books For Adults

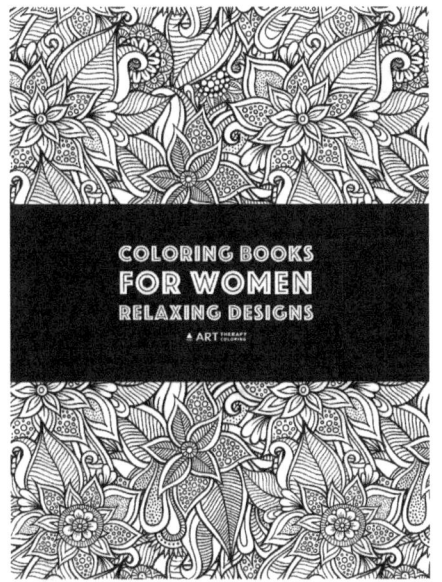

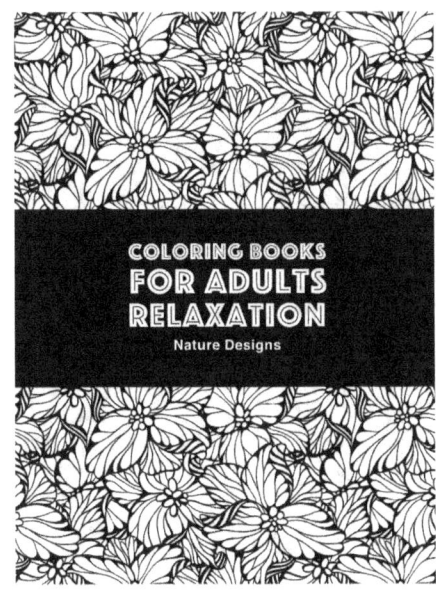

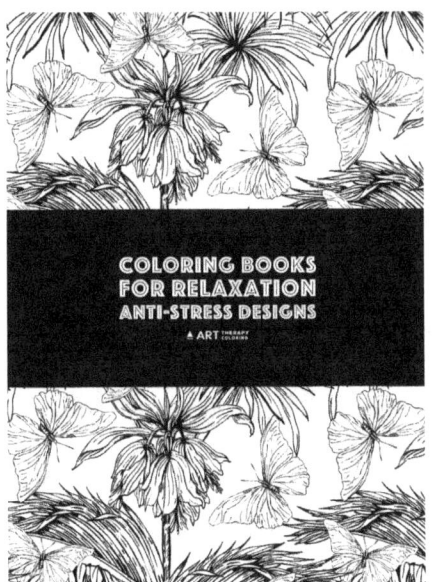

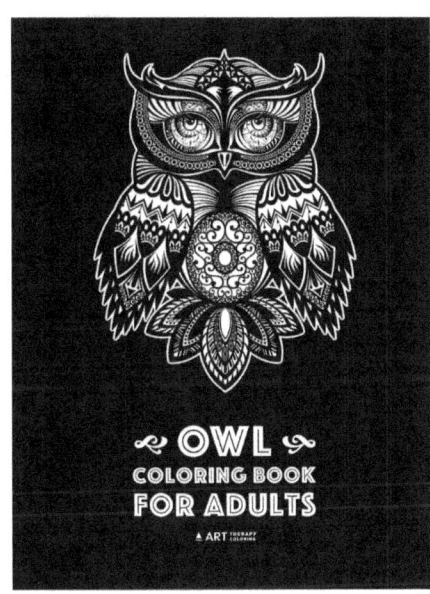

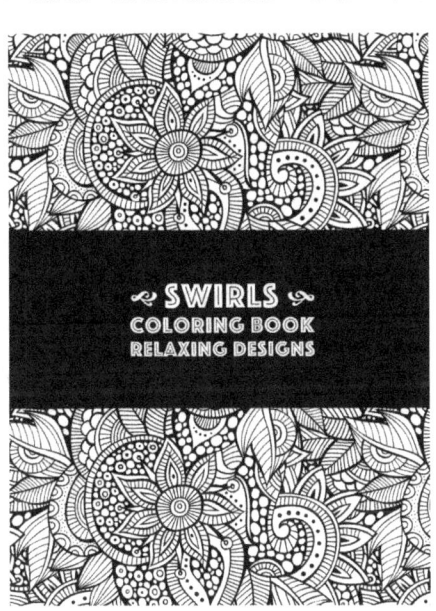

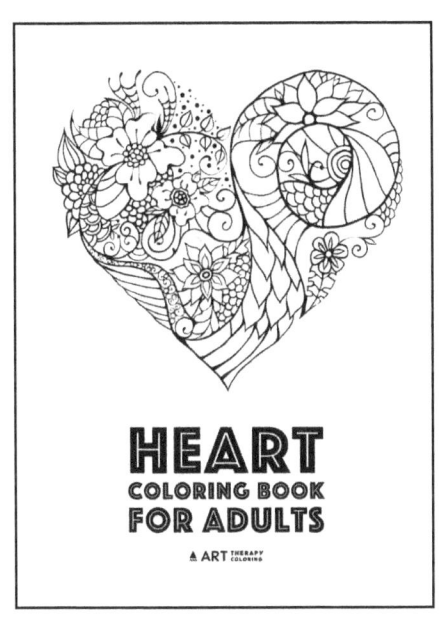

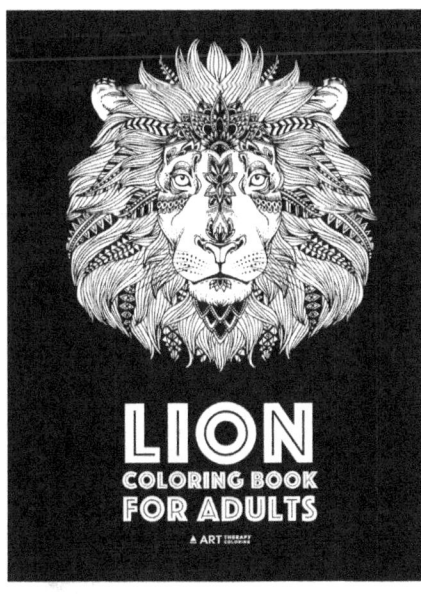

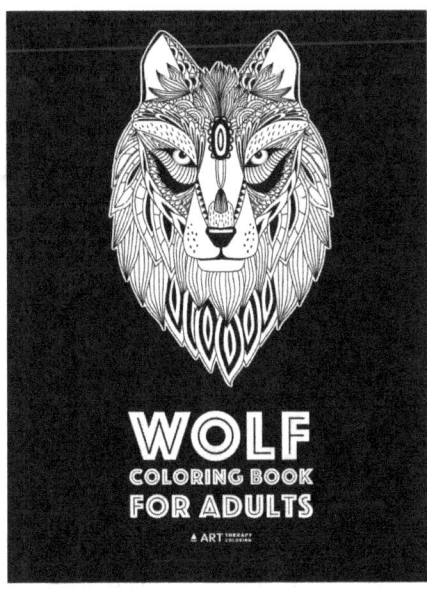

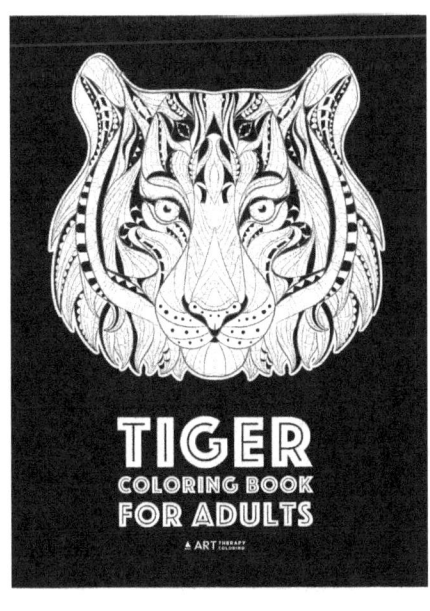

Coloring Books For Seniors

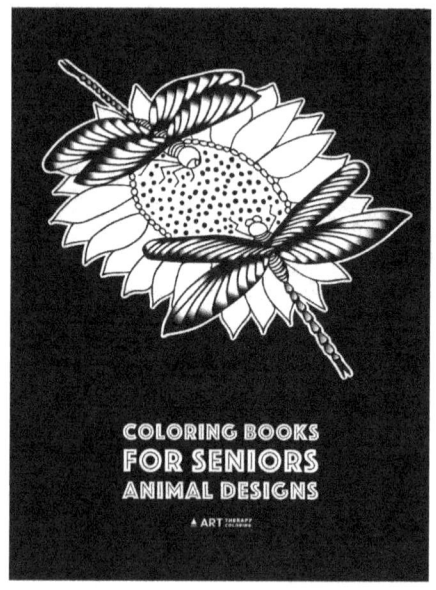

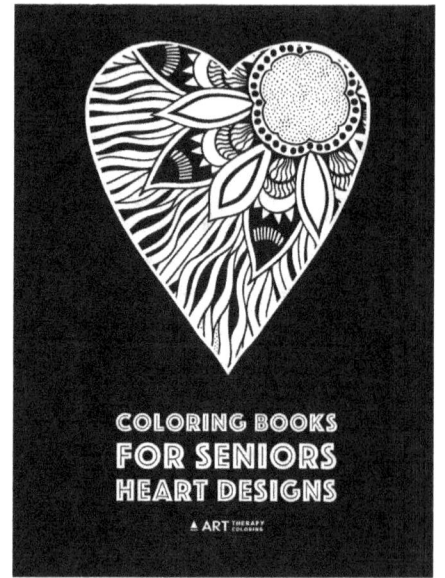

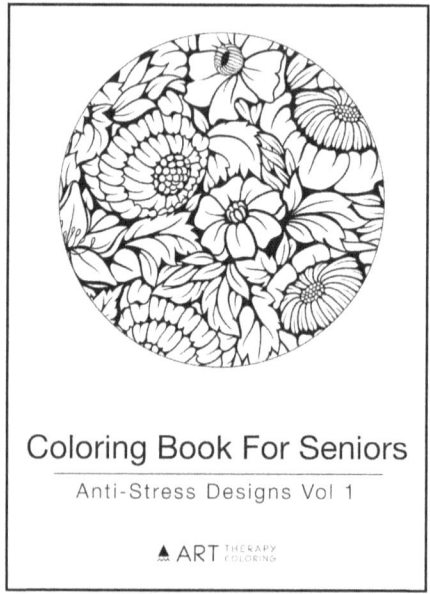

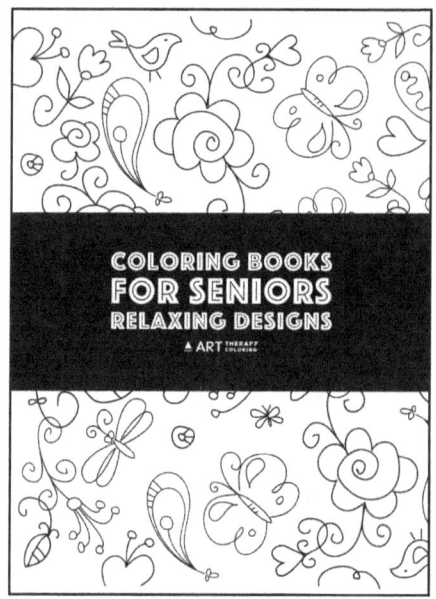

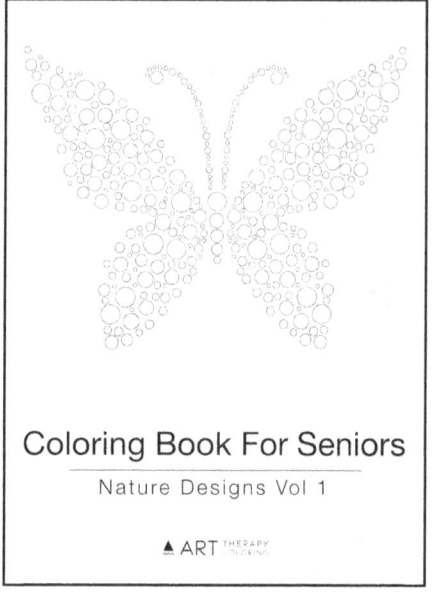

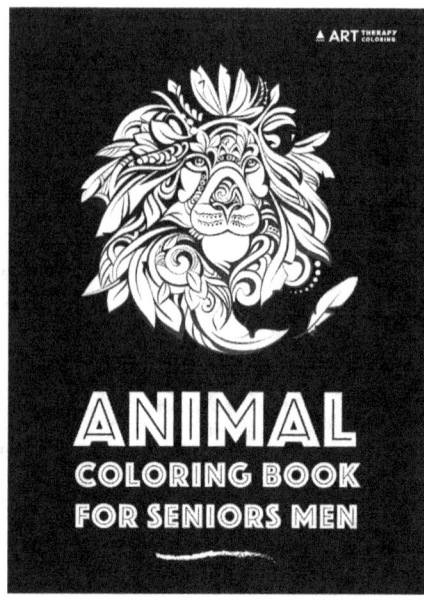

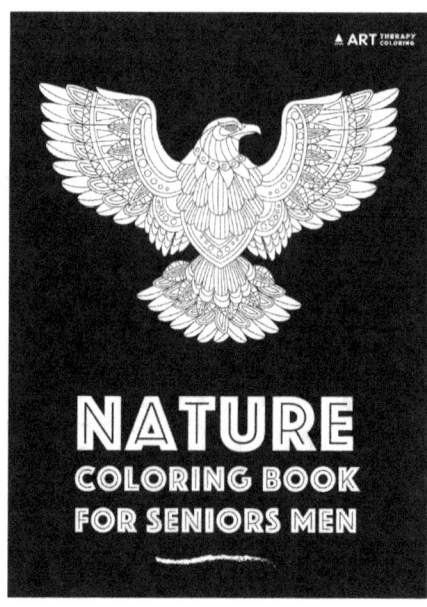

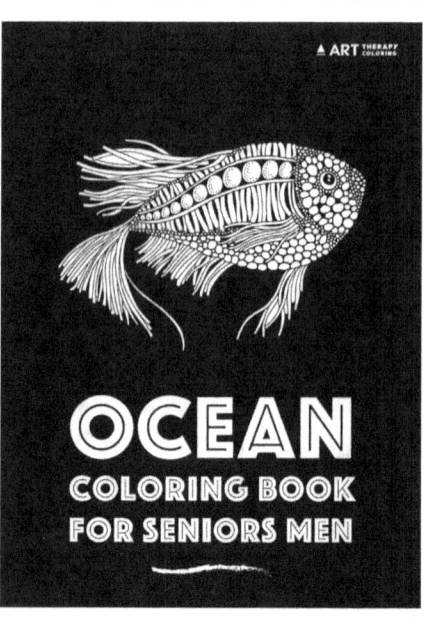

Coloring Books For Teens

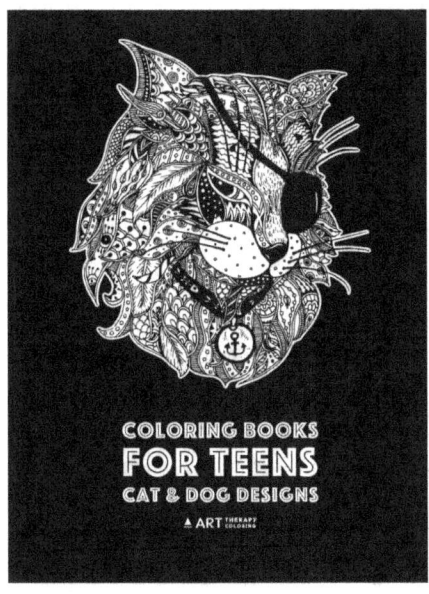

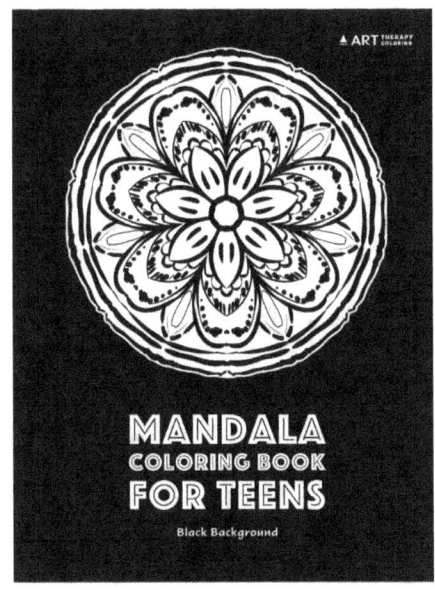

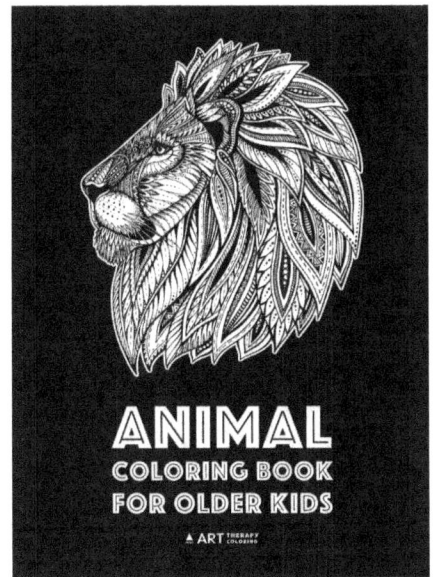

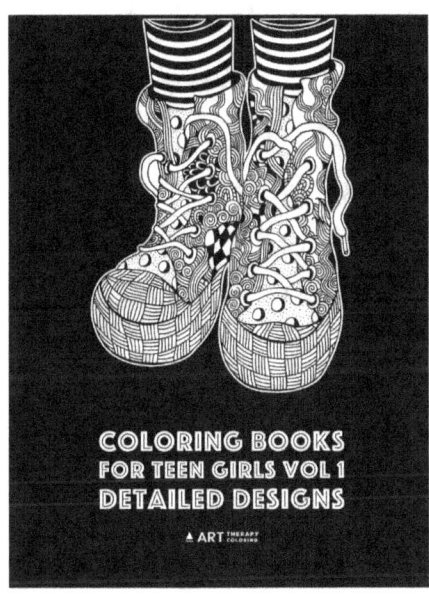

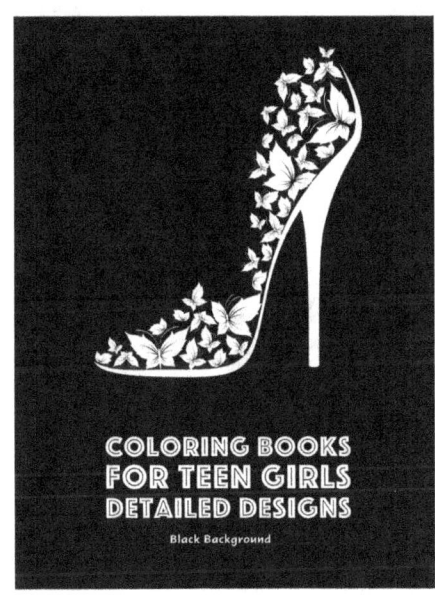

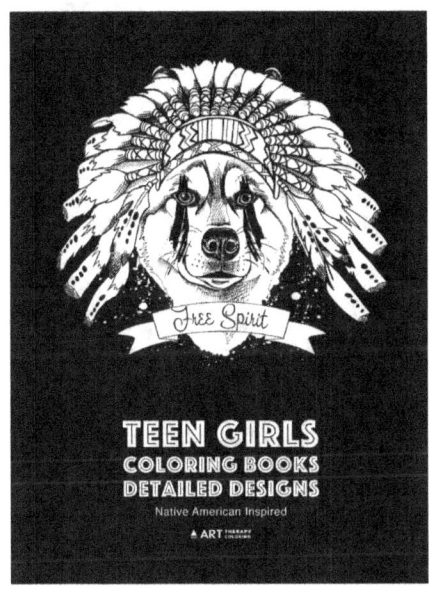

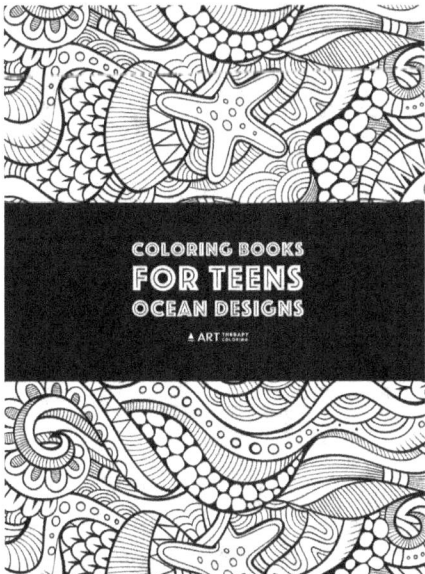

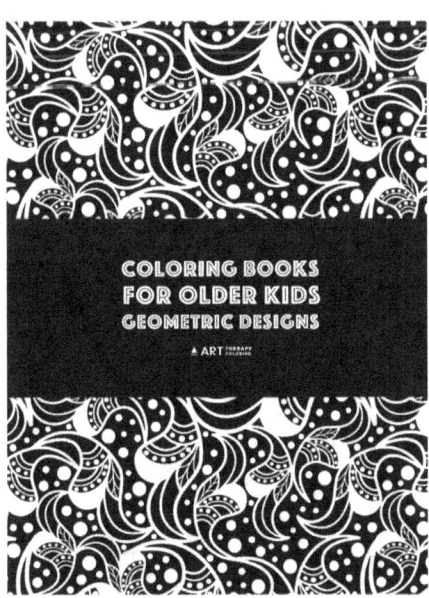

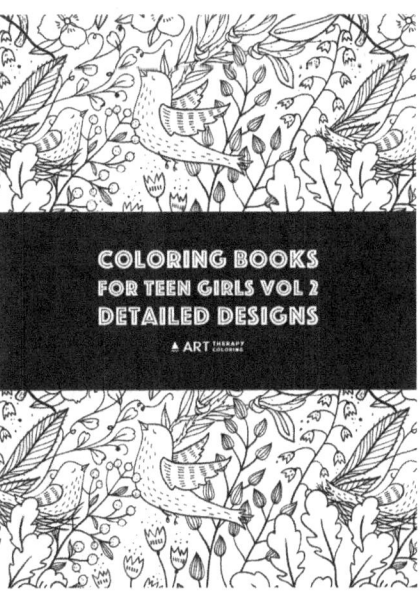

Coloring Books For Teens

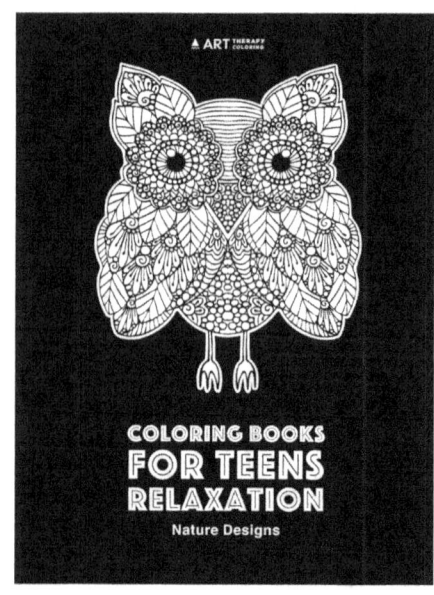

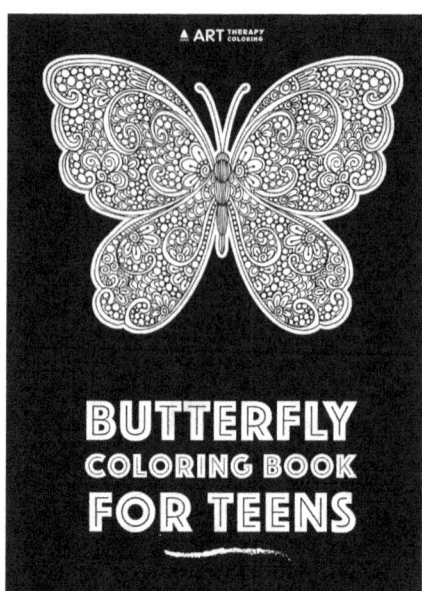

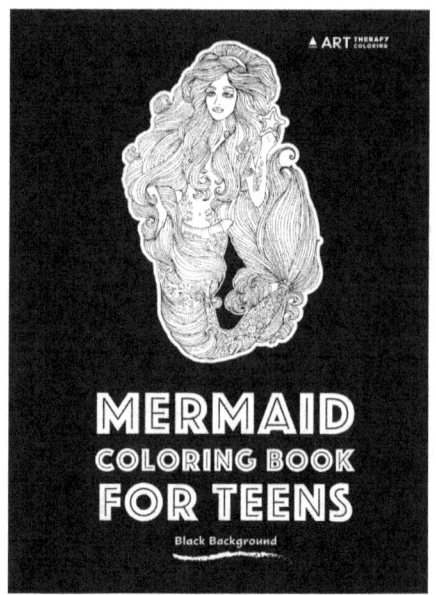

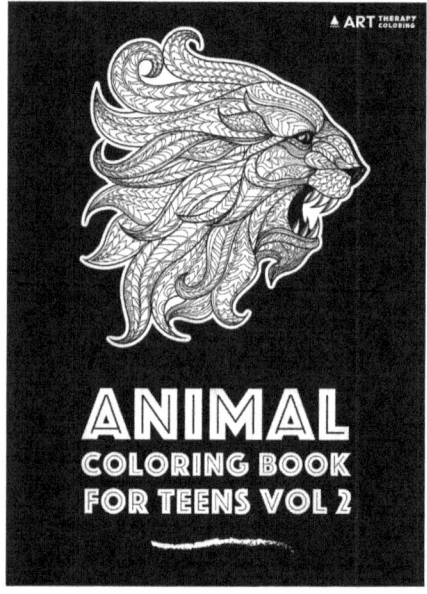

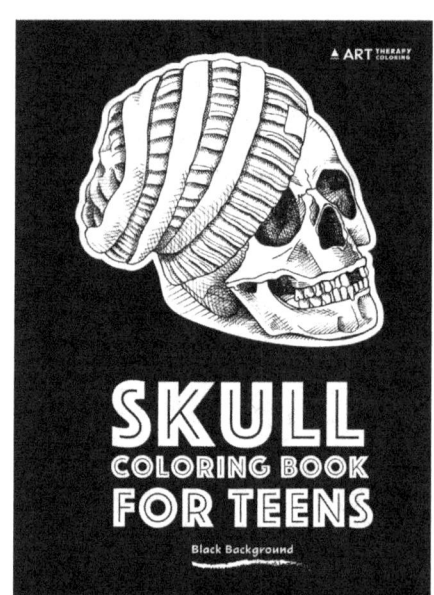

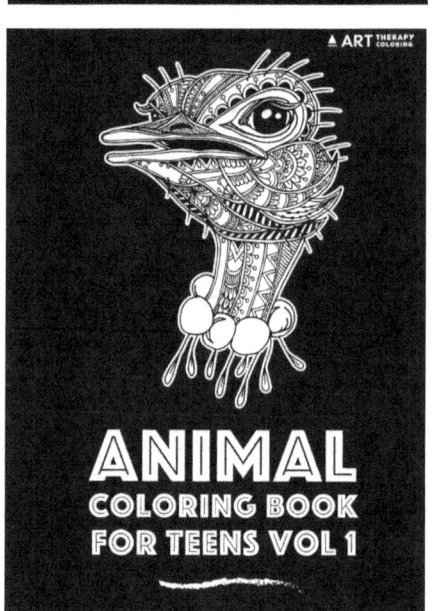

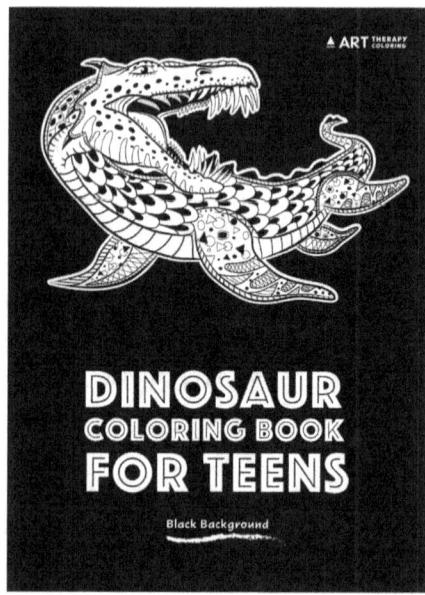

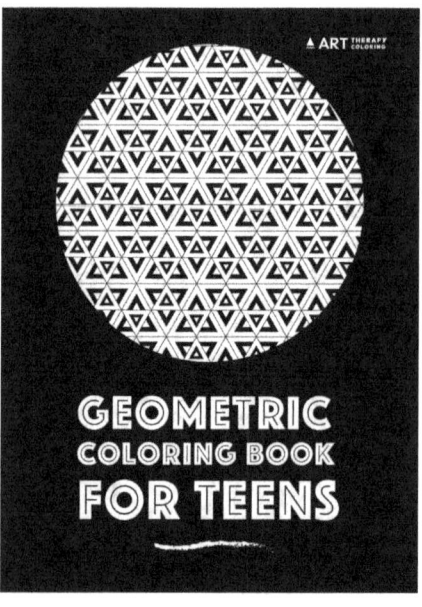

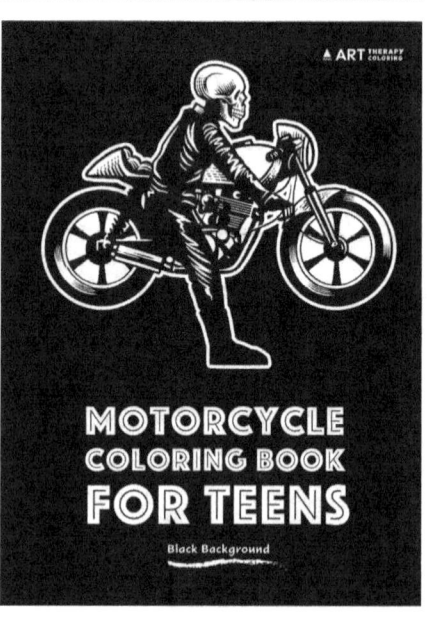

Coloring Books For Teens

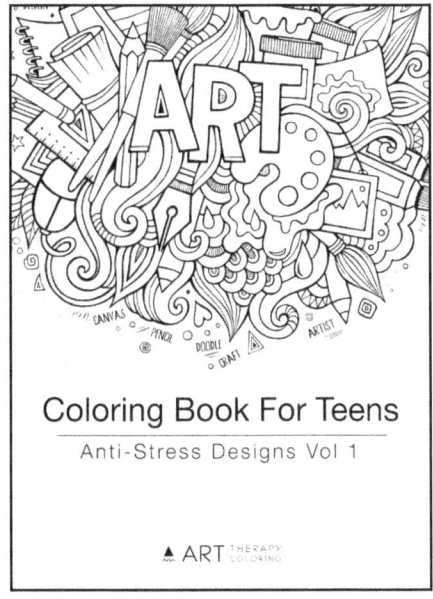

Coloring Book For Teens
Anti-Stress Designs Vol 1

▲ ART THERAPY COLORING

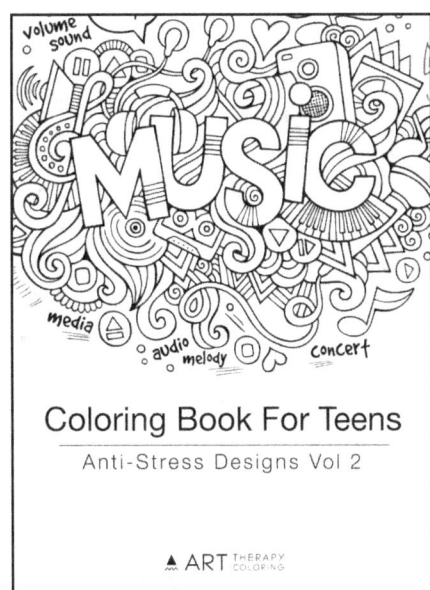

Coloring Book For Teens
Anti-Stress Designs Vol 2

▲ ART THERAPY COLORING

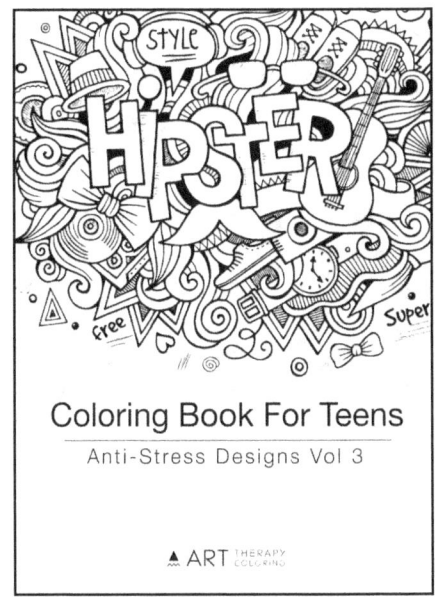

Coloring Book For Teens
Anti-Stress Designs Vol 3

▲ ART THERAPY COLORING

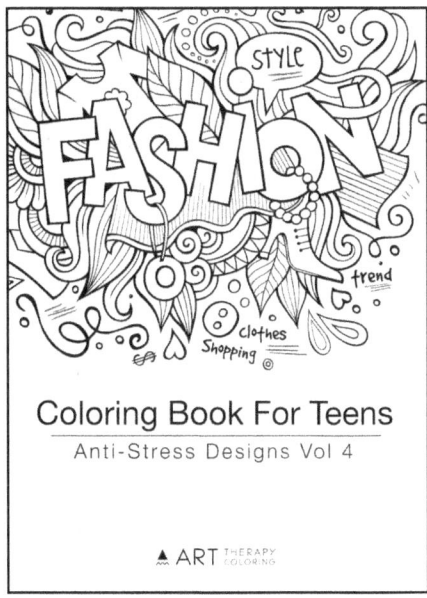

Coloring Book For Teens
Anti-Stress Designs Vol 4

▲ ART THERAPY COLORING

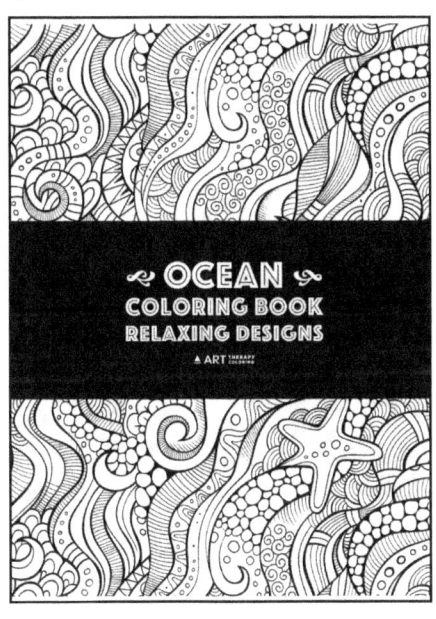

OCEAN
COLORING BOOK
RELAXING DESIGNS
▲ ART THERAPY COLORING

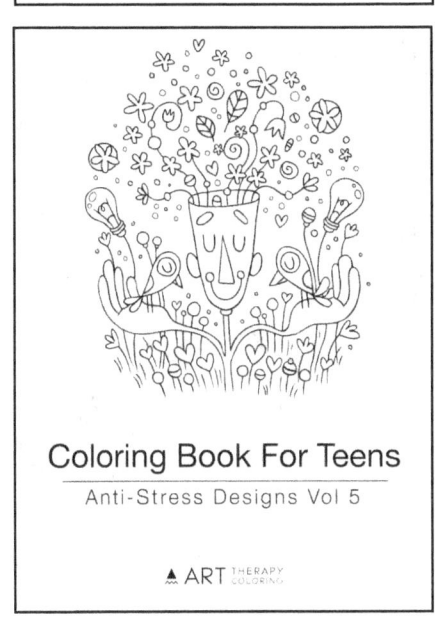

Coloring Book For Teens
Anti-Stress Designs Vol 5

▲ ART THERAPY COLORING

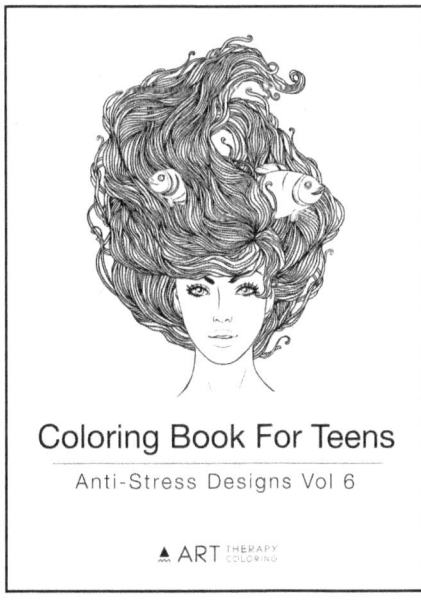

Coloring Book For Teens
Anti-Stress Designs Vol 6

▲ ART THERAPY COLORING

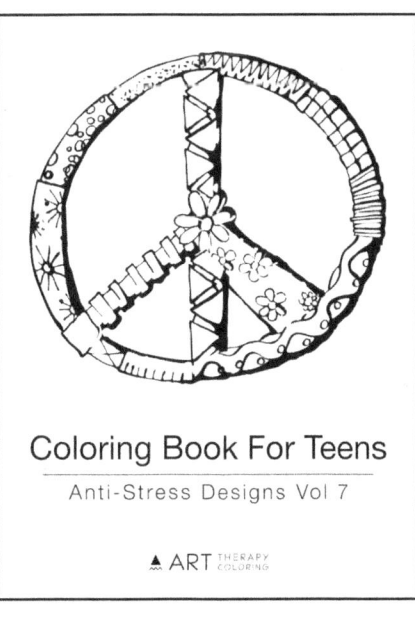

Coloring Book For Teens
Anti-Stress Designs Vol 7

▲ ART THERAPY COLORING

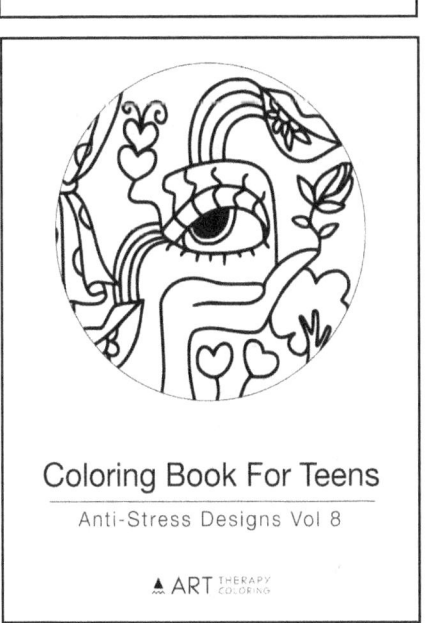

Coloring Book For Teens
Anti-Stress Designs Vol 8

▲ ART THERAPY COLORING

Coloring Books For Kids

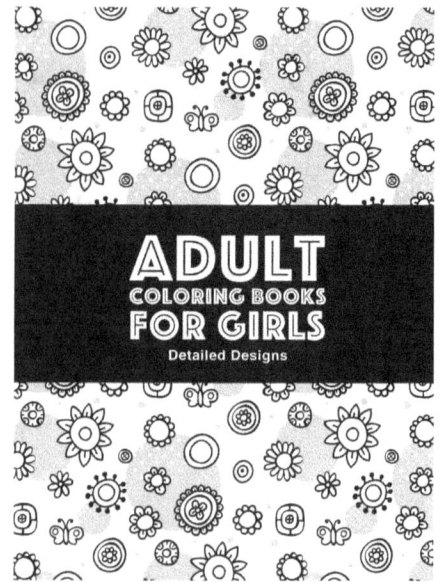

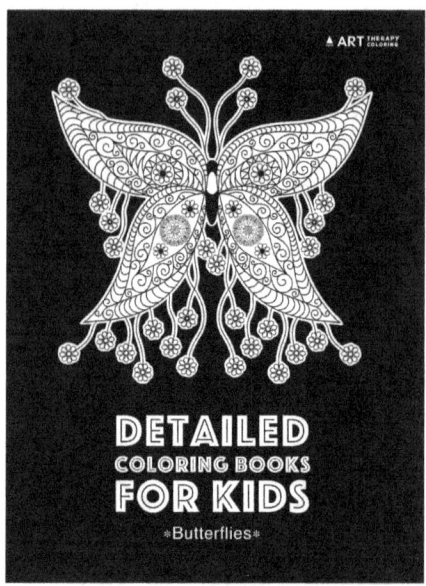

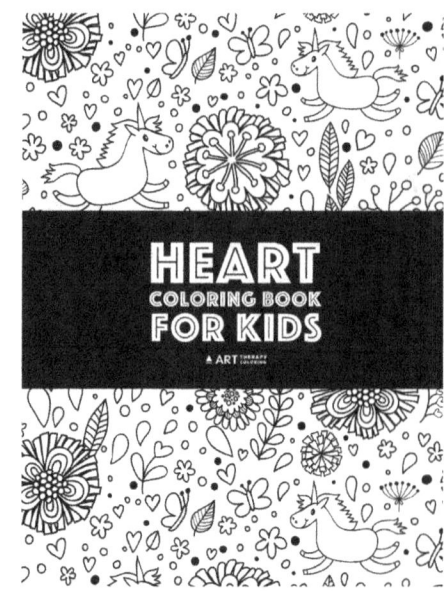

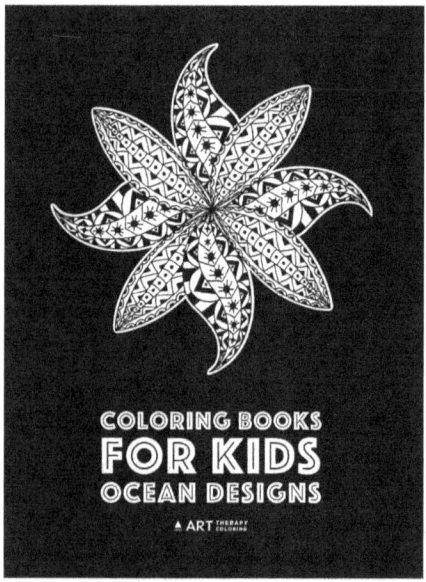

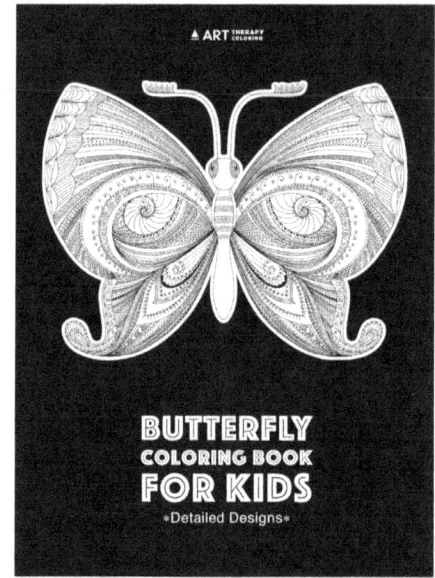

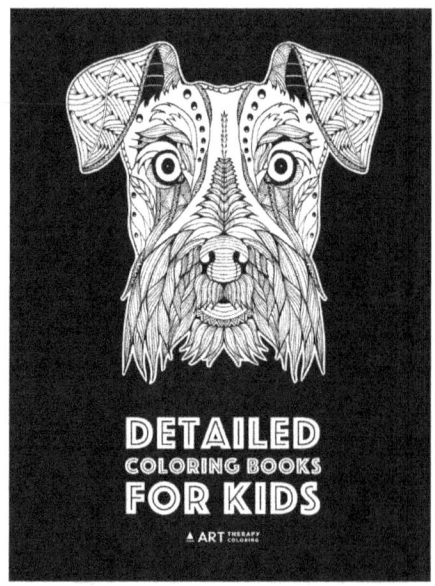

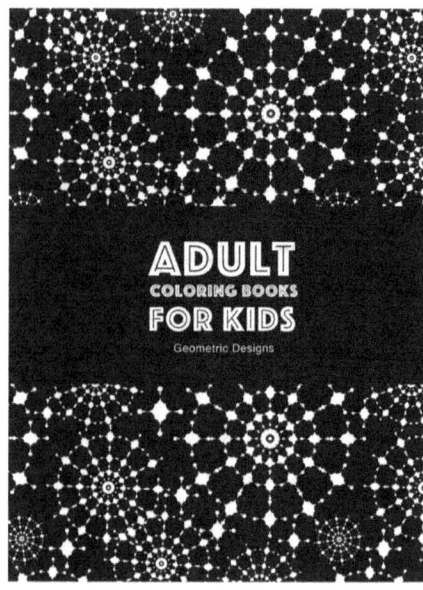

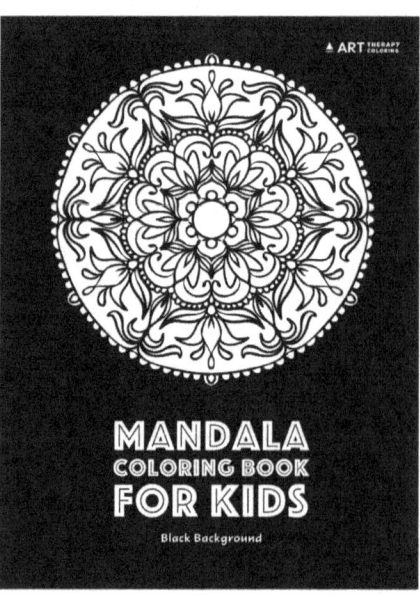

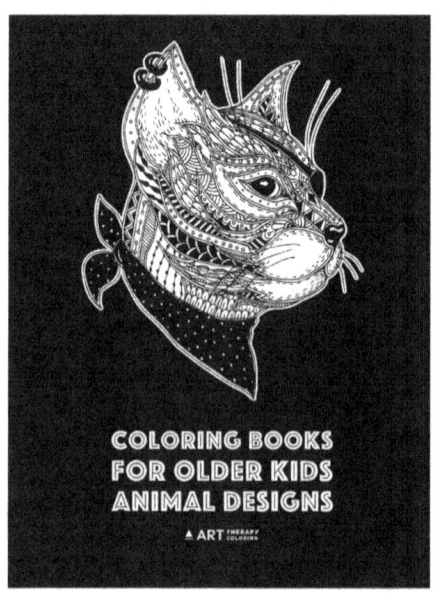

Coloring Books For Girls

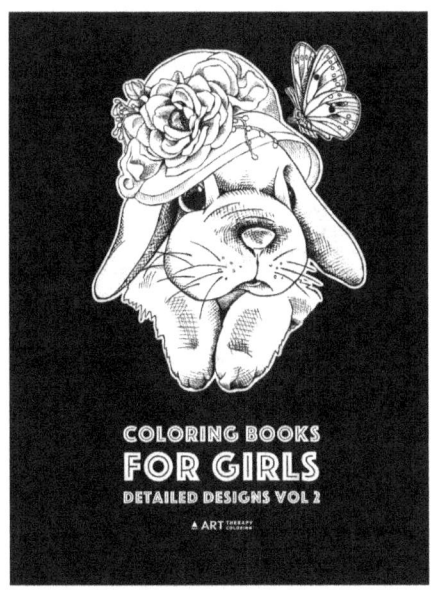

COLORING BOOKS FOR GIRLS DETAILED DESIGNS VOL 2 — ART THERAPY COLORING

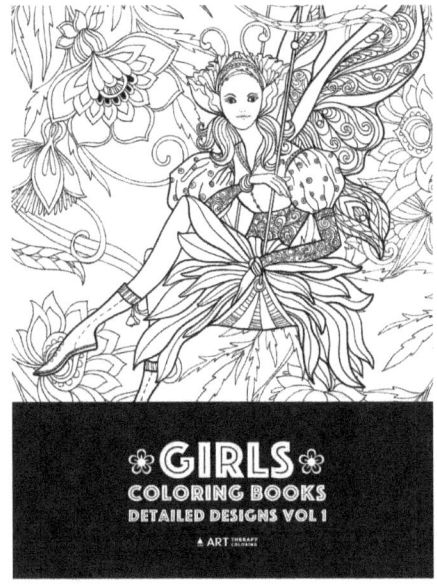

GIRLS COLORING BOOKS DETAILED DESIGNS VOL 1 — ART THERAPY COLORING

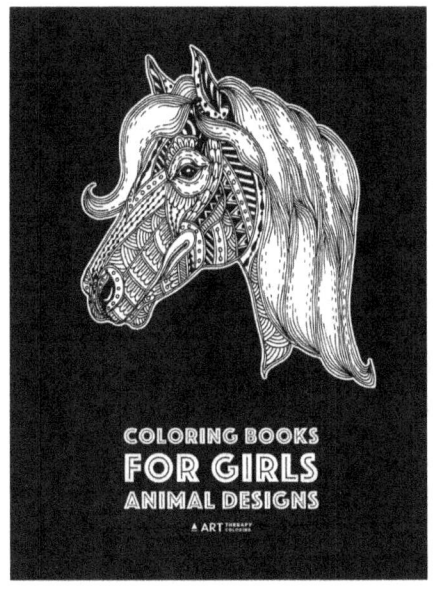

COLORING BOOKS FOR GIRLS ANIMAL DESIGNS — ART THERAPY COLORING

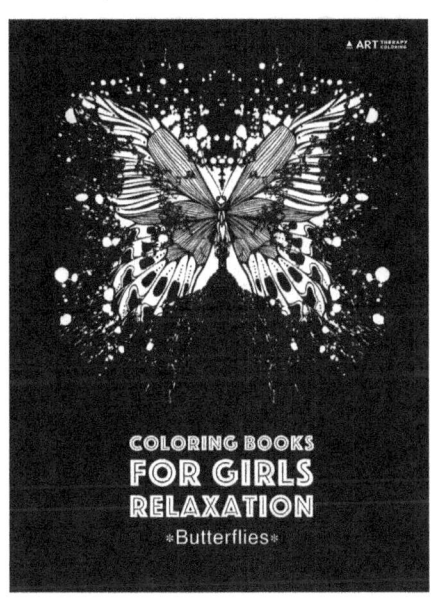

COLORING BOOKS FOR GIRLS RELAXATION *Butterflies* — ART THERAPY COLORING

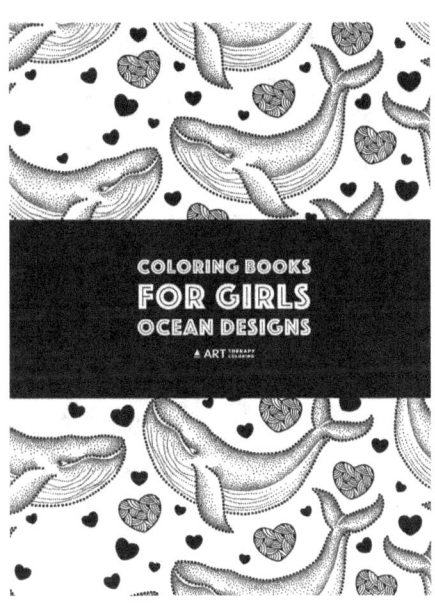

COLORING BOOKS FOR GIRLS OCEAN DESIGNS — ART THERAPY COLORING

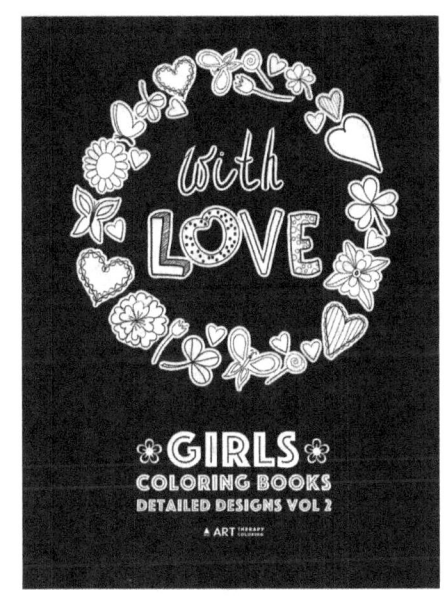

with LOVE — GIRLS COLORING BOOKS DETAILED DESIGNS VOL 2 — ART THERAPY COLORING

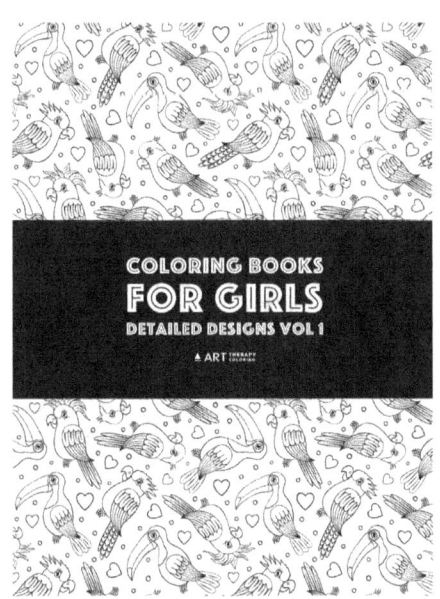

COLORING BOOKS FOR GIRLS DETAILED DESIGNS VOL 1 — ART THERAPY COLORING

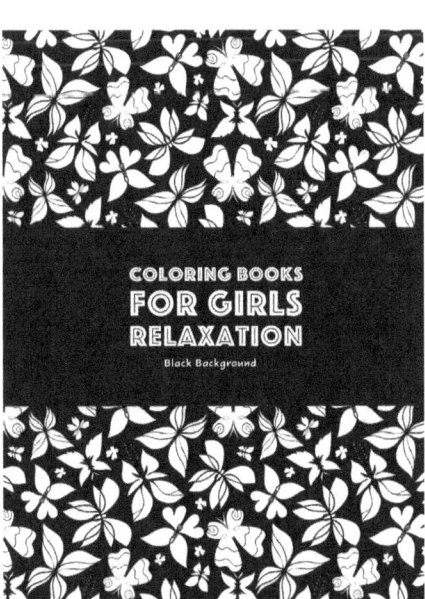

COLORING BOOKS FOR GIRLS RELAXATION Black Background

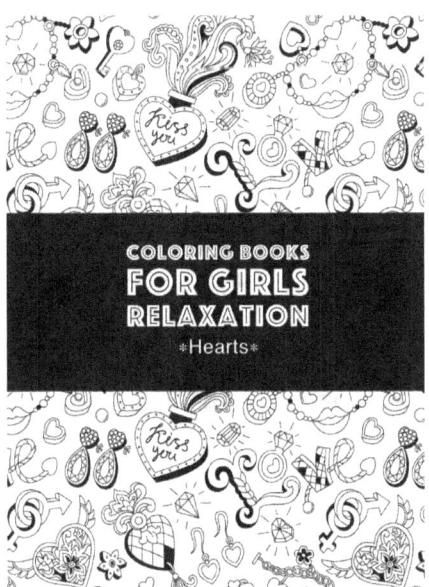

COLORING BOOKS FOR GIRLS RELAXATION *Hearts*

Coloring Books For Boys

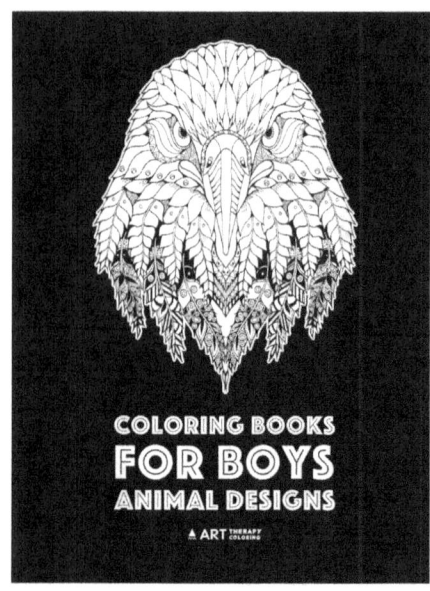

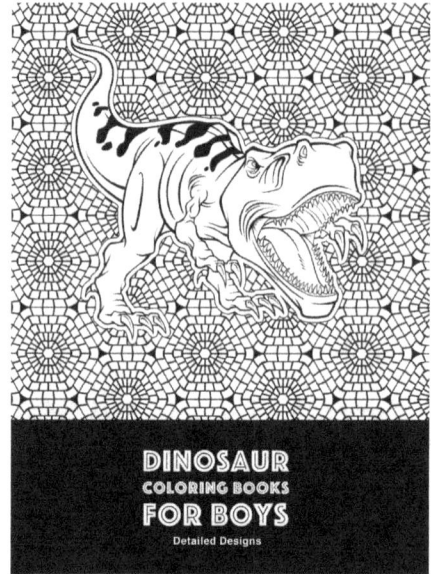

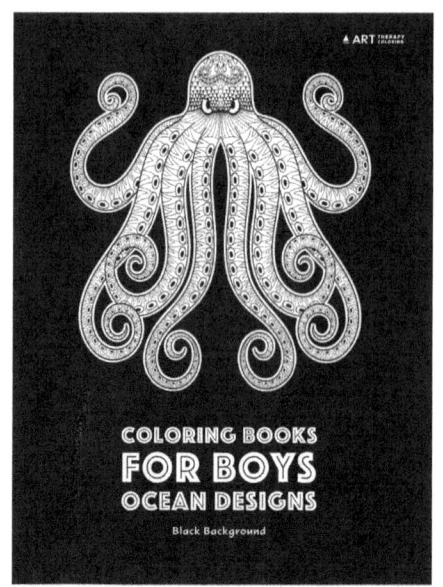

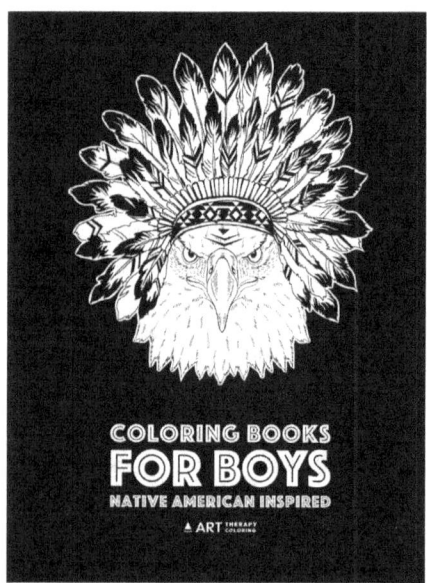

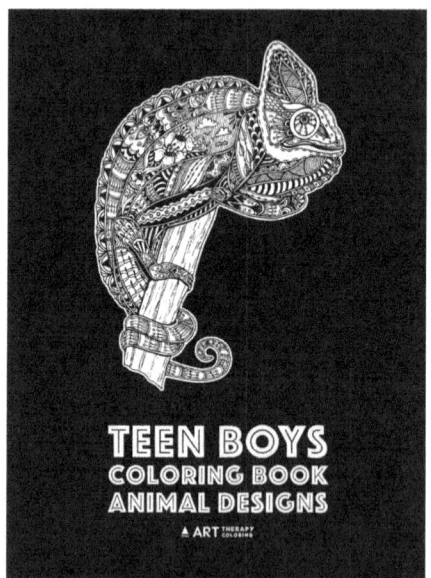

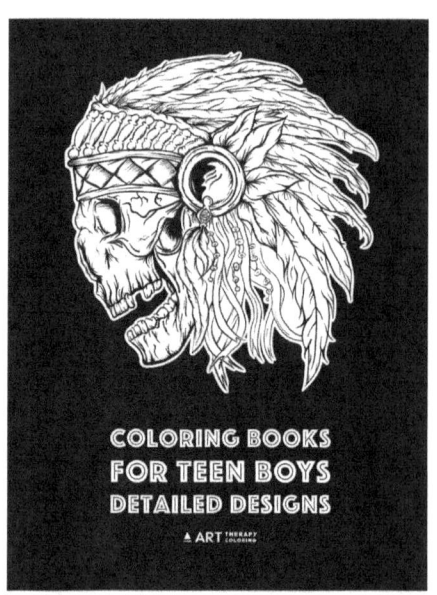

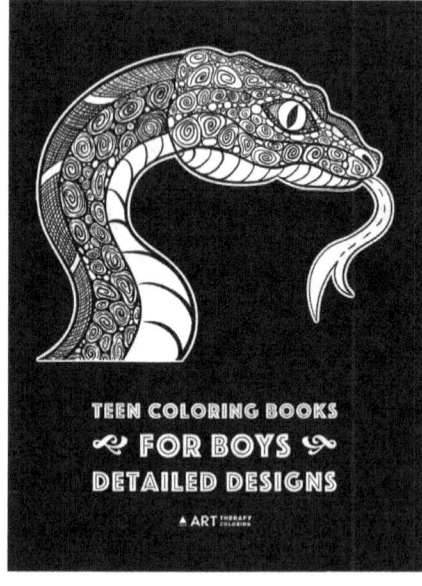

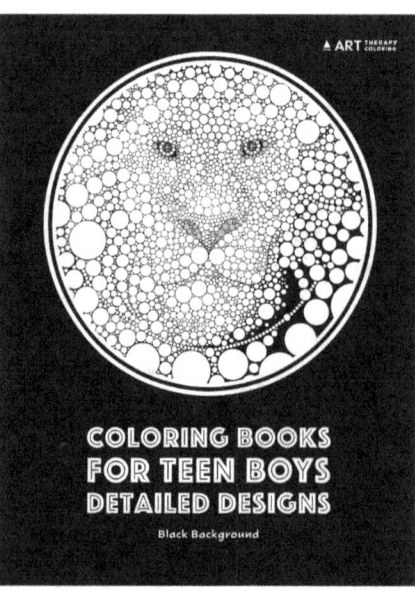

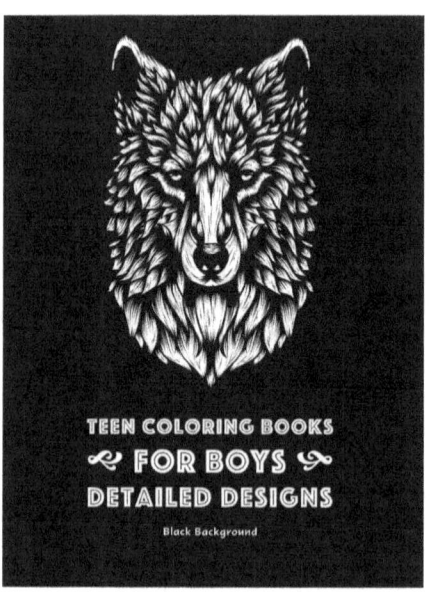

Coloring Books For Special Occasions

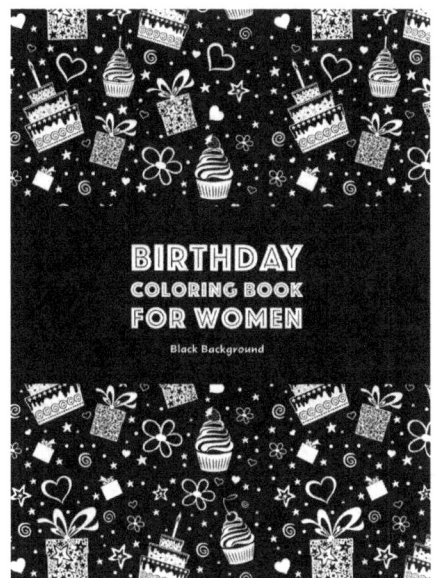

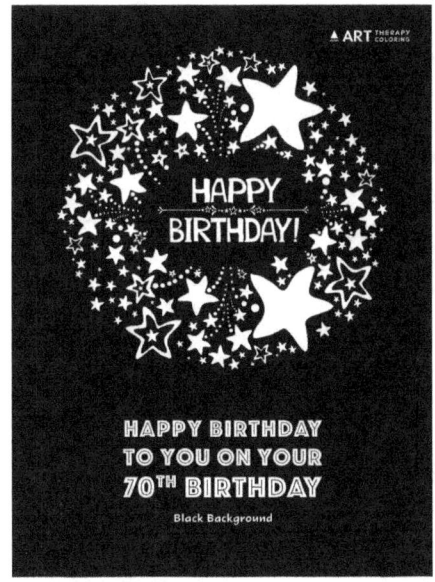

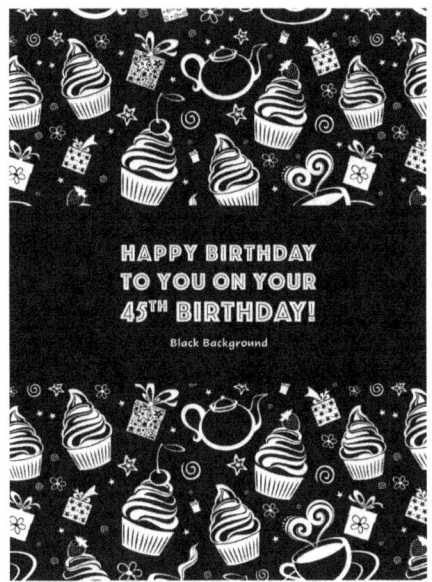

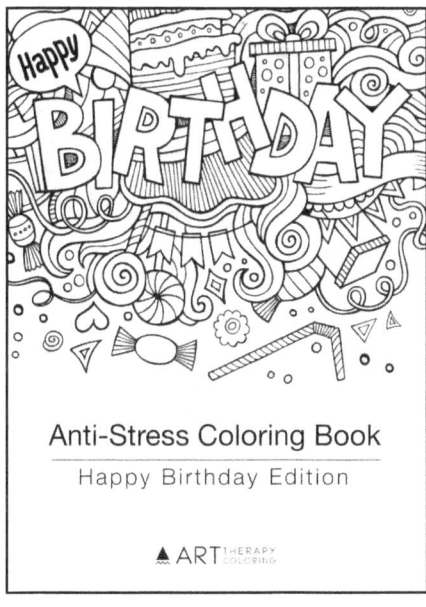

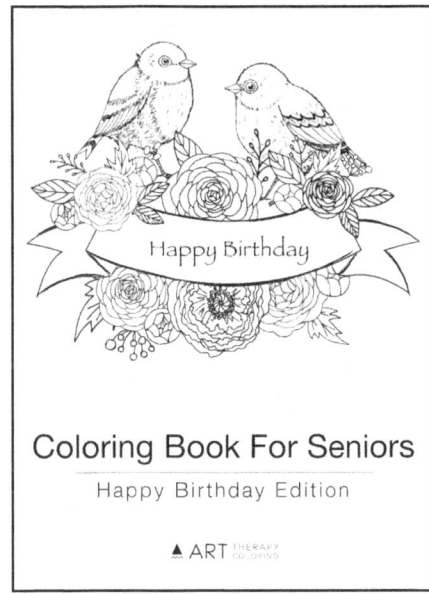

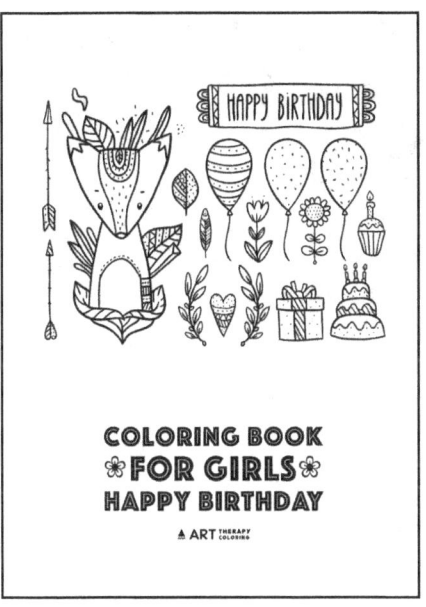

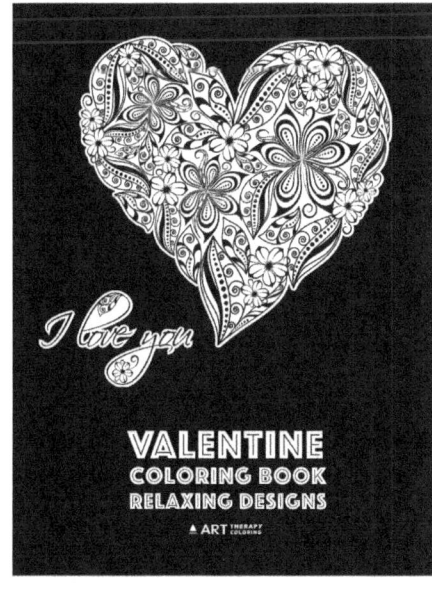

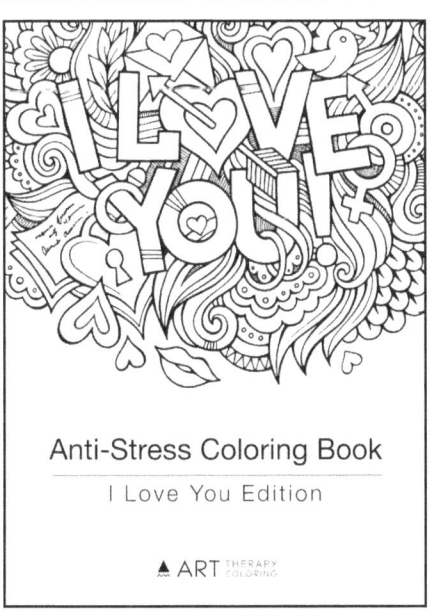

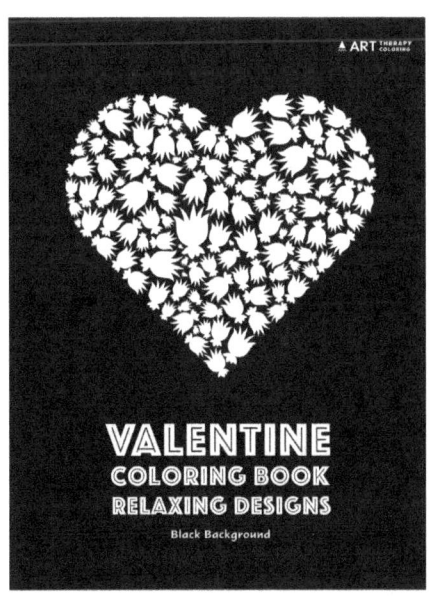

Coloring Books For Christmas

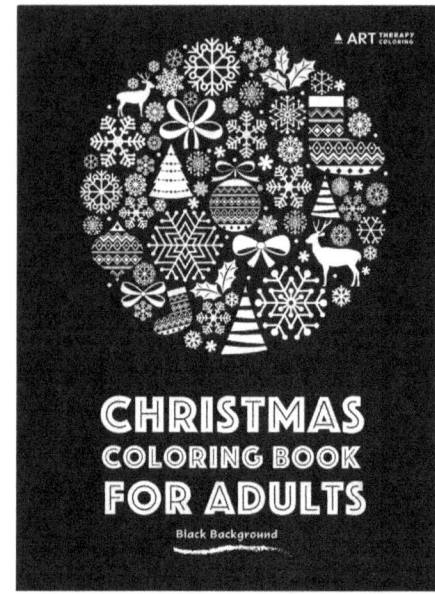

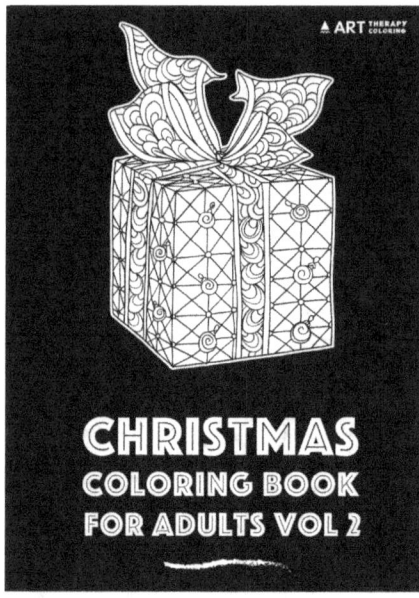

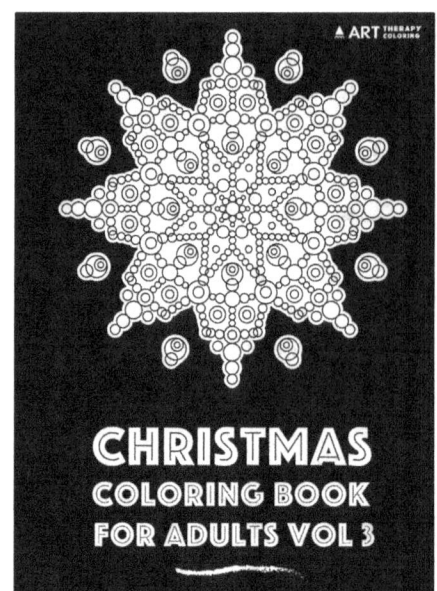

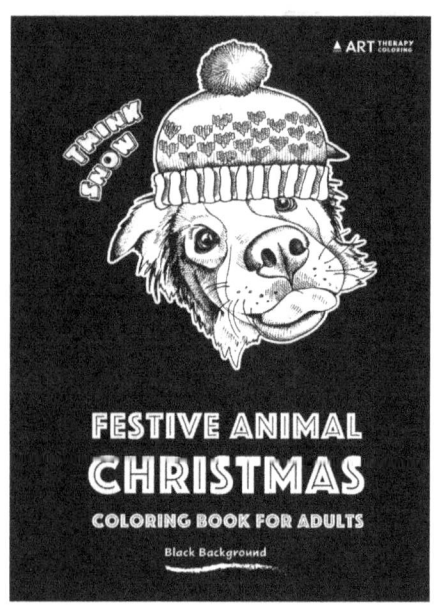

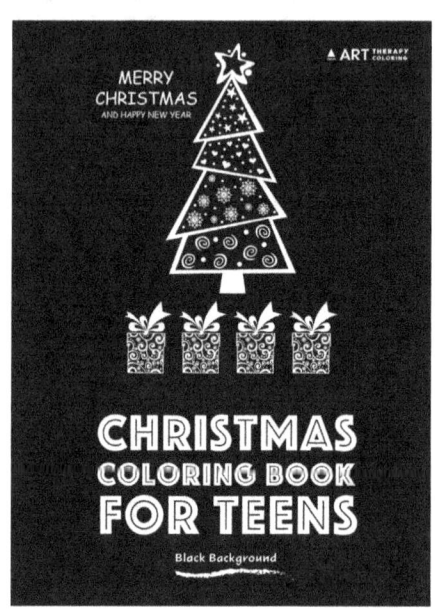

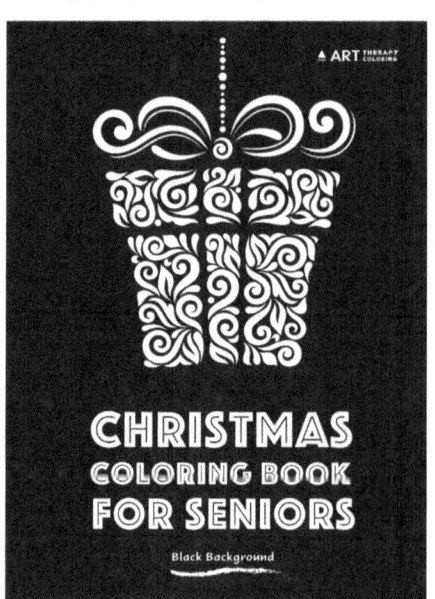

Coloring Books For Men
Hunting

Published by:
Art Therapy Coloring
El Dorado Hills, California
www.arttherapycoloring.com

Shutterstock Images

ISBN: 978-1-64126-011-4